001.307
Sch7j

87744

DATE DUE			
Mar 24 '76			

Joining the Human Race:
How to Teach the Humanities

Joining the Human Race:
How to Teach the Humanities

Fred E. H. Schroeder

To Jan and Erich

About The Author

Fred E. H. Schroeder *was born in Manitowoc,
Wisconsin in 1932, and, except for three
years in Panama City, Florida, he received
his public school education in his home
town, including two years at the local
normal school where he was trained as a
rural school-teacher. His first teaching
position was for grades five through eight
in a nearby village. From 1952 to 1960 he
taught elementary grades and junior high
school in several Wisconsin communities
while completing a bachelor's degree in English
at the University of Wisconsin during summers
and by extension and correspondence study.
During these years he also directed high school
dramatic and radio productions. In 1960 he
was a Woodrow Wilson Fellow at the University
of Minnesota where he received an M.A. in
English and in 1968, a Ph.D. in American
Studies. Since 1963, he has taught humanities
and American studies at the Duluth campus of
the University of Minnesota where he is presently
Associate Professor of English. His writings on
literature, art, biography, popular culture and
teaching have appeared in* Sewanee Review,
American Quarterly, Journal of Popular Culture,
English Journal *and other periodicals, and
several of his essays are currently part of
college writing anthologies. In 1969 he was
awarded a National Endowment for Humanities Younger
Scholar Fellowship, and in 1970 and 1971 he was
a writer, lecturer and journeyman humanist for the
National Humanities Series. An occasional museum
consultant for the National American Studies
Faculty, he also serves as one of the regional
presidents of the Popular Culture Association
and as a member of the Conference on English
Education's Committee on Teacher Preparation in
Humanities. He is currently writing books on popular
aesthetics and on educational projects
for museums.*

Portions of chapters II, V and VIII have appeared in the *Minnesota English Journal*, in the *English Journal* and in *Popular Culture and Curricula* (Bowling Green University Popular Press, 1970), respectively.

Contents

Foreword

As Professor Schroeder says, "the most dynamic force in American public education today is the 'Humanities' movement. . . ." In its three years of work in the midst of that dynamic force, the National Humanities Faculty can testify both to the excitement and the deep meaning which the movement holds for the present and future of our society. Yet as Professor Schroeder also points out, the movement's very groundswell nature has carried along its share of shoddiness and fadism with two chief results: First, that in some instances bad things are being foisted upon students, and second, that schools seeking to establish humanities programs often find themselves bewildered and puzzled as to how best to proceed. Moreover, the colleges need to rethink their own goals and to inaugurate programs to train humanities teachers.

The National Humanities Faculty has used its resources to bring outstanding humanists into schools selected on the basis of teachers' proposals to help attack these problems. This approach has proven highly successful; yet the very number of American schools has dwarfed the resources of the NHF, and we have for some time had in mind the potential to school and college people of just such a book as this. Without being dogmatic in the least, Professor Schroeder sets forth a rationale for the humanities, points out a number of worthwhile directions which a program might take, and discusses honestly some of the traps laid for the unwary.

The NHF takes great satisfaction in helping make available a work which grows out of Professor Schroeder's rich experience as a school teacher, a college professor, and a team leader in the National Humanities Series. Further, it is gratifying that this venture brings together several activities funded by the National Endowment for the Humanities. Their support has sustained the National Humanities Series and the National Humanities Faculty, and Professor Schroeder wrote the book as the recipient of an NEH Younger Scholar Fellowship. The author is a vibrant and devoted humanist who offers in this book the nourishing harvest of a unique set of experiences.

Arleigh D. Richardson, III

Preface

The most dynamic force in American public education today is the "humanities" movement, which initially grew out of various kinds of "Great Books" courses, but which has had influxes from a number of other contemporary movements in education. These boil down to two key words of the seventies, *relevance* and *interdisciplinary*, but they include such current enthusiasms as team teaching, modular scheduling, the inductive method, popular culture, the lively arts, minority studies, and nondirective teaching. There is great energy and excitement in these approaches to education, but they are too frequently marked by faddishness, superficiality, and lack of discipline.

This book is an attempt to unify the different directions and emphases that these new approaches have engendered, particularly where they have fallen under the catchall term *humanities*. My approach in each of the ten chapters is to set forth the problems inherent in the methods, to build a rational philosophic base for instruction, and to provide some suggestions for lessons and curricula. The problems and the philosophies are universal, and although most of the patterns I provide are initially aimed at secondary school humanities teaching, I suggest ways in which the patterns can be adapted to all courses and grade levels.

The material in this book draws upon my two decades of teaching experience at all age levels, from primary grades to graduate schools; and it is presented from a highly personal point of view because, as I explain in the last chapter, a personal style is essential to creative humanities teaching. On the other hand, the entire book is an argument for clear-headed, responsible scholarship as the firm base upon which humanities courses must stand.

I thank the National Endowment for the Humanities for the support provided me by the Younger Scholar Fellowship that I was awarded for 1969-70. My thanks, too, to Norman Ross and Arleigh Richardson for their encouraging interest in the original manuscript of this book, to Mrs. Nancy Clemente for her incalculable help in readying it for publication, to Marie Knope for typing the early drafts, and to my wife, a humane critic and a most critical humanist. Finally, a blanket thanks to all the teachers and students whose brains I have picked over the years.

F.E.H.S.

I
Humanities for Everybody:
Plugging into the Human Race

Rather conveniently, Neil Armstrong landed on the moon while I was leading a "workshop" in the teaching of humanities. His landing was timely because the members of the workshop and I were trying to arrive at some fairly acceptable definition of humanities as a current movement in American schools, and we were wrestling with questions of the purpose of the humanities approach to learning. Being something of a cynic as well as an opponent of journalese, I was venting my irritation at the endless flow of drivel about "Man" and "Mankind" emanating from television's daily philosophers. It was not "Man" who landed on the moon, I complained. It was Mr. Armstrong—who, as it turned out later, seemed to support my view by amending his statement that his act was "one small step for man and a giant step for mankind" to read, "One small step for *a* man . . . ." It was not *We*, I argued, but *He* who landed on the moon, just as it was not Europe or mankind that had landed on San Salvador Island in 1492, but *a* man, Christopher Columbus.

But my students disagreed with me. They were right, and

if I was not humbled, I was most certainly enlightened. The ultimate purpose of humanities, they said, was to help our students join the human race. This is the true brotherhood of man, to feel sometimes that we all share in the achievements of great men, explorers and of pathfinders, because they are men as we are men. This is why the humanities approach in the schools of the world is so urgently needed, because so very many people are not card-carrying members of the human race. For some in slums, ghettos, jungles, and tundra, the membership cards have been withheld. Therefore, for me to say that I do not share in man's achievements is self-indulgent cynicism of the most perverse sort, but for a malnourished girl in a filthy shack in Appalachia to say that she does not share in the achievements of mankind is a cruel fact of existence—one cannot say a fact of life, for what is there of life when one is denied membership in humanity?

For others, though, those whom E. E. Cummings called "manunkind," the membership cards have not been denied, but spurned; spurned because of conceit, because of cupidity, because of cruelty, because of bigotry. Possibly, in his heart of hearts, manunkind realizes that the membership card entitles one not only to the rights and privileges of humanity, but to the common guilt of mankind as well. Accept the moon as yours, and you must accept the pollution of the earth as yours too. Accept what is ennobling in the schools and the religions of the world, and you must also accept with it what is narrow-minded and bigoted, shallow and unfeeling. To extend E. M. Forster's *mezzo-voce* cry, if we claim to be members of the human race, we can only say, "Two cheers for humanity"; two cheers, because of the brotherhood of guilt. In what is otherwise one of the most dreadful poems in the English language, Michael Wigglesworth's Puritan diatribe "The Day of Doom," there is a poignant scene wherein the spirits of unbaptized children appear before the throne of New England's God to protest their damnation. They plead, "Not *we*, but *he*, ate of the tree"; and the Great Administrator replies in the vein of that unrelenting edict of *The New England Primer* which says: "*A* is for Adam: In Adam's Fall *We* Sinned All." We share the guilt of all humanity, for we are indeed our brothers' keepers.

But let us not wallow in that guilt. And, most particularly, let those of us who are humanist teachers not employ shared guilt and *The New England Primer* as selling points for the humanities. If we are to redeem the dwellers of the deepest slums and shallowest suburbs, we cannot purchase them with guilt and gloom, for we are part of Neil Armstrong's achievement not because we have sinned, but because we are human beings, and potentially we are as great as any. I am a part of mankind's greatness because I matter. Or at any rate, I think I matter.

Cogito, ergo sum: Which brings me to humanities in its traditional sense as it appears in the great works of Renaissance Humanism. Descartes's famous conclusion funnels all the problems of philosophy down to one being, one human being who matters. Beware, though, of reverence for great quotations, for if you read this as meaning "Descartes thought, therefore *he* was," you haven't plugged into humanities or humanism or the human race. What Descartes's statement means for me personally is *I* think, therefore *I* am; what it means for me as a teacher is that it is my task to make every student say it too, so that he also matters. The humanities teacher says *you* think, therefore *you* are.

There's a catch here, however, in the word "think," because if you don't think, why then, you simply ain't. That's where teaching comes in and that's where the teacher comes in, and that's why I have written this book. Humanities for every student is a noble goal, and it may be the hope for the redemption of manunkind, but no one can really plug into the humanities until he thinks. Very well. But even for teachers of the loftiest vision, the question remains: "How?" How does one make the student think, and think like a member of the human race? To answer this question, I will in this book descend frequently to matters of nuts and bolts, brass tacks, and nitty-gritty. I will do this because my interest is in humanities for all students, and to reach them it is necessary to concentrate on the basics. The humanities, or liberal education (the two are interchangeable), are for thought, enjoyment, and understanding, and these should not be the exclusive domain of a cultural elite. Elitism in the humanities is what leads to "Descartes *thought*, therefore he *WAS.*"

But, to quote Robert Frost, "as I was saying before Truth broke in," the heyday of humanities was in the Renaissance. The revolution in the ethos that made it possible for Descartes to conclude *cogito, ergo sum* affected many men who expressed the idea of "man that matters" in many forms. Shakespeare's tragic heroes, Lear in particular, are men that matter, not always because of their strength or social heroic stature or achievement but because they are men who think, and therefore are, and therefore have dignity because they matter to themselves. Faust's voracious appetite for knowledge is part of the revolution, too, for it is man thinking bigger than he is, and that matters. Leonardo da Vinci's science and technology presume to control nature, and in that respect, Leonardo's view of the world assumed that nature was there for man, who matters. In Renaissance painting, scientific perspective assumed that the world exists in the point of view of man. Thus when Filippo Brunelleschi stood in the northwest corner of the Piazza della Signoria and painted what he saw from his perspective, his perspective mattered because he mattered. The world of Renaissance art is measured in units of man, and Renaissance men did not see themselves as small units. Michelangelo's Adam, for example, is an elevation of man to his highest potentialities. He is not the Adam of *The New England Primer*, but the Adam of man made in God's image, and such a man matters.

Note that Michelangelo's Adam expresses iconologically the heightened potentialities of man, not a celebration of his achievements. This point is important for the teaching of humanities, because it must be recognized that the ultimate goal of the teacher for his students is potential, incomplete, and open-ended. The purpose of the humanities teacher and, so far as the word is applicable, the humanities "course" is to make each student aware of his potentialities as a human being. How and to what degree he realizes his potentialities is his business, and this fact is what makes humanities teaching not totally satisfying. The completion of the course—whatever period of time that may represent—is the commencement of the real course, and the real final examination is life itself. Ultimately, humanities is a course of questions, not answers, and this fact, too, is dissatisfying, to both teacher and student. Compounding the dissatisfaction is the knowledge that the basic questions of the humanities have never been satisfactorily answered, and possibly are quite unanswerable. But they are not forbidding or aristocratic questions; they are relevant questions, because every man has the potential power to deal with them. The catch, once more, is that he must *think* if he is to know that the questions exist. This is dissatisfying, too, because, for one thing, it is more comfortable not to think, and not to cultivate questions at all, than it is to construct a tentative world of doubts. The humanist's world may promise exalted potentialities, but it has never promised roses.

I, though, did promise nuts and bolts. Exactly what are these questions and where are they to be found? Some are perennial, the heritage of our past. What is man? Who am I? What is man's purpose? What is man's duty? But in most cases, the questions are neither so grand nor so general, and they are anywhere and everywhere, just where you find them. Look back over the paragraphs above, and you will find I have planted a litter of significant questions. For example, I said my students were right and I was wrong about whether or not the moon was conquered by a man or by mankind. Is my final judgment true? Is it true that we all

share in the achievements of mankind? Was Neil Armstrong a
hero or a tool? What is a hero? Are heroes needed?

Is it true that the child in Appalachia or the urban slum
has been denied membership in mankind? If it is true, can
this case be remedied? I rather glibly put the dwellers of
jungles and tundra in the same bag with the dwellers of
slums, rural and urban alike. Is this just? Does material
poverty mean cultural poverty? Is the Amazon Siriono or the
Alaskan Eskimo outside of humanity? Because their lives
would not satisfy me, are their lives unsatisfactory in toto?
On the matter of guilt, is there truly a common guilt of
mankind? Is it inherent in man or is it imposed by each
culture, or is it individually achieved? Are we our brothers'
keepers? Who are our brothers? How do we "keep" our
brothers?

There are more specific questions, too. A matter of
aesthetics: Is "The Day of Doom" one of the most dreadful
poems in the English language? What can *dreadful* mean?
What is a good poem? "The Day of Doom" is a sincere poem.
Has sincerity anything to do with aesthetics? A matter of
history: What is the Renaissance? Does it exist at all in
reality? Are there truly historical epochs? A matter of
philosophy: What is meant by *cogito, ergo sum*? Is it really
wrong to say, "Descartes *thought*, therefore he *was*?" Are
not things in the past simply in the past? And is it mere
vanity for me to say that I matter because I think I matter?
Doesn't everyone think he matters? How about that Eskimo?
How superficial are my remarks about the Renaissance? Are
the terms *humanities* and *liberal education* really interchangeable? Is it true that the humanities need not be elite? Do all
men have the same potentialities? Are all men created equal?

All these questions are worth asking, and none seems to
be the kind of question that can ever be absolutely answered.
But in every case some kind of answer can be given from a
base of common sense and everyday experience, and in that
respect they are questions for humanity. And, furthermore,

in every case some more extended answer can be given from a background knowledge of history, art, metaphysics, literature, logic, and current events; and in that respect they are questions for the humanities. This brings me to the pressing matter of relevance, not only of the humanities, but of the whole fabric and technique of education. These questions are relevant, because they relate to every man's life. That is why they can be approached with common sense and daily experience. And these questions are what can make all knowledge, not only of the present, but of the past, relevant, because they are perennial questions. Get caught up in these questions, and you get caught up in the human race—and a long race it is—because the perennial questions make us contemporary with all men who have pondered the questions. We can thereby be contemporary not only with Neil Armstrong but with Descartes, who is, not was.

Of the questions above, however, only the last three are relevant to the subject of this chapter, and these are therefore the only ones on which I will essay an answer. As a professional teacher in America, there is only one possible answer for me, and that is that all men are indeed created equal, that we all share the same potentialities, and that the humanities need not be an elite study. Yet no one can be so innocent as to believe in the practical equality of men, for we all recognize the most obvious inequalities of birth, for instance, in the dramatic case of brain damage. Further, anyone who has taught elementary school children knows that the varying capacities for learning are as often the result of created inequality as they are of imposed or learned incapacity. That is to say, it is perfectly clear that in all children, to some degree, intelligence is inherited. On the other hand, it is common knowledge that inherited incapacity or weakness is often augmented by environmental deprivation, that is, a restricted exposure to cultural and social experiences. In addition, we now know that even when the environmental deprivation is remedied, there may persist a psychological posture of incapacity, and this state of mind operates with a devastating feedback. The child thinks himself unable to learn as well as others, and so he does not learn as well as others; and he begins his next day one more step behind, his incapacity and inequality confirmed in fact. This state constitutes a psychological analogue to "I think, therefore I am" in that one is, psychologically, what he thinks he is. That is why the underlying concepts of Renaissance humanities are so desperately important. The exalted image of Michelangelo's Adam and the Promethean appetite for achievement and knowledge of Faust are icons of man's potentialities that must be believed in by all men, regardless of inherited and environmental inequalities. The icon represents a mythical truth, not an empirical truth, but if the humanistic myth can abolish the unwanted nonempirical inequality of the psychological block to learning, we are one bit closer to the realization of the myth.

In this general sense, therefore, humanities is a powerful educational means for destroying the ghetto consciousness. In America, however, the ghetto consciousness is often black consciousness, and a lily-white Italian Adam of centuries past is remote, foreign, and, if anything, a confirmation of inequality. But there are black images of equal majesty in the powerfully realistic statues of Richmond Barthe and the black and white drawings of Charles White. Leave it for a later time for black children to take pride in and measure their potentials against the great works of traditional African art; let them first see that Black is Beautiful in heightened realism, just as white men learned in the heightened realism of the Renaissance that Man, as they knew him, is Beautiful.

But even if this goal can be achieved, we must still contend with inherited inequality of capacity for knowledge. Universal public education is not, and can never be, an equalizing institution within the traditional disciplines. Many a master of arithmetic is incapable of mathematical thinking; many a mathematician could never be a bookkeeper. Keen and accurate memory is essential to achievement in many disciplines and vocations, and memory ability varies greatly. Manual dexterity is also an unequal gift, and some electronics industry executives are doubtless incapable of working on their own assembly lines. Few people have genuine drawing ability. And I have met scientists who appear to be congenitally unable to think in metaphors. In fact, I have even met humanists for whom metaphorical thought is the product only of painful training, and for them, the empirical tastes of indexing, collating, and teaching historical surveys are far more congenial than interpreting or making humanistically relevant works of art. This all sounds as if I am demonstrating in the most unequivocal fashion that all men are created *un*equal. Look back, though, and you will see that the instances of created inequality are all vocational. They relate only to what men do in society, not to who men are in society.

Most educational institutions are almost solely vocational schools, and all educational institutions are sometimes vocational schools. That is why destruction of equality is one of the main side products of schools. When inherent variations in the capacity to learn to read separate a first-grade class into three reading groups, vocational education has begun, and it will continue throughout the educational process. In America, however, the disintegration of equality through vocationalization will be accelerated quite humanely, beginning in the junior high school years, when free elective courses are made available, and in high school, where college-preparatory and non-college-preparatory divisions will be made on the basis of variable ability to cope with verbal and symbolic vocations. In America, too, the educational institutions will attempt to hold some kind of equality in required courses in English, history, and social problems. But too often these required courses are vocational courses, more or less thinly masked. In senior high school, the English courses are often composed of histories of English and American

literature; history courses are compilations of data, thrice
separated from the reality of historical events by means of
secondary-source textbooks and teachers' notes copied from
lectures read from professors' notes gleaned from other
secondary sources; and social problems courses are frag-
mented reports of current events, much less interestingly
presented than television newscasts, which one would turn
off if they were as drab as school.

Colleges, too, give a nod to humanistic studies and equal
education, but, as often as not, the required science and
mathematics courses are used to weed out nonmajors. Art
and music departments disguise vocational studio and performance courses with general titles. And when freshman
English courses begin to lean toward the humanities, the hue
and cry is set for vocational training in grammar and
footnoting.

Do not think, though, that I speak as an enemy of
vocational training, nor even as an enemy of inequality. I
applaud the separation of students on the basis of ability all
the way from the three first-grade reading groups to the
division between M.D. and Ph.D. Like Diogenes looking for
an honest man, I'm searching for a better trained auto
mechanic, a more efficient bibliographer of humanistic
articles, and a better prepared loophole-finder at the H&R
Block tax office. My purpose is not negative, but positive. I
am an advocate only for true education in the humanities, an
education that makes all of us brothers in mutual respect, in
dignity, and in delight in being members of the human race.
As a teacher and writer, I too have an interest in vocational
training. I want to prepare professional humanists and I want
to find a place in the curriculum for the humanities and for
humanists. But the vocational purpose is only part of my
interest, for the ultimate purpose of humanities education is
the preparation of *amateurs* in the humanities. Let every man
and woman be a true professional in his vocation; but let
every man and woman be a true amateur in this lifelong
avocation.

The plea for keeping the humanities in balance with vocational education is particularly strong today, but it is not new to the modern world. Renaissance Humanism, insofar as it was an educational movement, expanded the largely vocational character of medieval training of the clergy, yet the Renaissance neither wanted nor achieved humanities for all the people. Even when so complete a humanist as Thomas Jefferson pressed for greater relevance in his reforms at William and Mary and the University of Virginia, he directed most of the relevance toward vocational goals: modern languages, scientific agriculture, and diplomacy. The controversy that raged between Thomas Huxley and Matthew Arnold in nineteenth-century England was essentially a battle between vocational training for the masses and humanities for the masses; and the C. P. Snow-F. R. Leavis quarrel of the 1950's was similar. Today's plea, however, may be more urgent, for we are now, in our schools and colleges, confronted by the products of more than a decade of almost exclusive vocational training of the most insidiously chauvinistic sort and suffering the effects of an attitude toward education completely destructive to the ideal of the unity of mankind.

On a warm October night in 1957, my wife, my infant son, and I sat on our porch, watching Sputnik I tumbling and winking across the sky. At that time, my wife was an elementary school librarian and I was a junior high school teacher of mathematics and art. And, at that time, we felt strangely part of the great achievement of men in reaching for the stars, in freeing man from gravity as only artists like Michelangelo had ever done before. But had we known at that time what devastating meaning the new satellite would have for American education, we might have despaired, for it sicklied over an educational system that—in spite of its manifest weaknesses, its inefficiency, the shoddy intellectual training of teachers, the jargon-ridden education school establishment, and the whole pall of anti-intellectualism that afflicted our schools—had in the century before 1957 strived continuously toward equal, and relevant, and humane preparation of children for life. Sputnik seemed to us that October evening to promise more, not less, confidence in humane and pertinent education. But what Sputnik evoked in our nation was not pride in humanity but an attitude of "beat the Russians."

We did beat the Russians, as the opening words of this chapter indicate, but we apparently found, too, that being members of mankind meant more than nationalism. But at what a cost! Beat the Russians: learn Russian. Beat the Russians: start mathematics earlier. Beat the Russians: cut out the arty frills. Beat the Russians: make education more *efficient*. Replace chatty men with chattering machines. Place high school and college students before a television set. Give more homework. Separate the best students into elite accelerated classes, where they can do college level work, which means research papers, footnotes, and homework, and more homework, and never a question of beauty or of human dignity. It is no wonder that the young people today are rebelling. They have been trained efficiently, with note pads on armchairs, facing a blue television screen; with earphones clamped about their heads in little boxes in language laboratories; with three-by-five note cards and footnote stylesheets in libraries; with computerized final examinations; with legalistic "contracts" for learning "at their own speed," all alone, horribly, anonymously alone, and totally unrelated to the others around them, all pathetically isolated, tied only to their contracts to learn one more thing more efficiently and more unequally. It is no wonder that the products of this nightmarish system shout for relevance, march for mankind, attack their teachers, and pursue chemically-induced sense experiences. They want to join the human race, and that's where humanities comes in. There is not really a problem of whether or not humanities for all students is possible; of course it is possible, since its questions have built-in relevance and can be approached with no more background than common sense and personal experience. The problem is only that the student must be made to respect his own common sense and personal experience, while the teacher must respect the student for what he is; and at the same time the teacher must strive to open windows on wider cultural and intellectual horizons. But how, specifically how, can teachers help every man to get in giant step with Neil Armstrong and mankind?

II
Where Angels Fear to Tread:
Planning the Humanities Curriculum

Some years ago I was hired to teach junior high school "core," a curricular term that antedates the more sophisticated-sounding "humanities." What I was expected to do was to teach American history and English. Because I rather prided myself in having an integrative mind, I envisioned a perfectly dovetailed, integrated course in which my students would study the history and the literature of given periods and places in American life, whereupon they would exercise their learning in freewheeling writing assignments. But I failed to do as I had intended, and ultimately I divided the two-hour period evenly between history and English. If inexperience combined with youthful enthusiasm makes one a fool, I think now that I was an archetypal fool who rushed in where angels had feared to tread. But now, with the angelic credentials of a Ph.D. and six years' experience in teaching college humanities courses, I know a little more about why angels may have feared to tread where I had rushed in. Furthermore, I now see a spate of problems involved in planning any kind of humanities program in any kind of school.

The first of these problems is one that has been solved only by Faust—hardly an example to follow. The problem is that one can't do everything. Nevertheless, given the fact that anything in the story of mankind can be grist for 'the humanities teacher's mill, all humanities teachers tend toward a Faustian drive to try to do everything, and they want to do it all in the academic gestation period of nine months. The Faustian drive is not in itself bad; indeed, it is necessary if one is to have faith in human potentialities, but it must be curbed and channeled to meet the very practical demands of education.

The modern humanities movement in American schools goes in many directions, and, it is to be feared, too often it goes in all directions at once. The modern humanities movement is opposed to the traditionally narrow disciplines of knowledge, but it is to be feared that because of this renegade purpose, too often it becomes undisciplined in the process. The modern humanities movement emphasizes the student-centered approach to wisdom, but, in so doing, it too often becomes puerile and unsophisticated. The only hope for remedy for these distortions and exaggerations is in the teacher, who must have an intellectual base, a body of knowledge, and a sense of direction. This does not mean that the teacher must be restrictive or pedantically disciplined or must possess several angelic doctorates. What it does mean is that *someone* in the humanities classroom, discussion group, or field trip must not be lost, regardless of what directions may be followed.

There are several bases upon which the humanities teacher and his curriculum may stand, but I think there is no better base than the Renaissance. First, it is a base that swivels between the old world and the new world, both in the sense of the Ancient World and the Modern World and in the sense of the strictly European world and the new, global world that followed Columbus. Second, the Renaissance gave birth—or rebirth—to the concept of humanities as a way of life and a theory of education. Furthermore, it is in the Renaissance concept of humanities that the primary characteristics of modern humanities received their most emphatic statement and definition, so far as definition is possible. It is not my purpose, however, to set forth any fast definition of humanities, nor is it my purpose to outline any precise or ideal curriculum of humanities for public schools or colleges; for, more than anything, humanities is an attitude—a way of thinking about—teaching, learning, and life. Nevertheless, some base is needed, and at least a moot definition is desirable, so that teachers, students, and, it is to be hoped, parents will have some common ground of understanding. One valid definition of "humanities" is that it is the study of the humanities, that is, the arts and social studies. The inclusion of social studies is debatable, but when it is considered that many works which are by any definition humanistic (Plato's *Republic*, More's *Utopia*, Castiglione's *The Courtier*) are also unquestionably "social" studies, it seems clear that any humanities course of study must include both the arts and the social studies. The distinction between these definitions of "humanities," however, is easily resolved if we regard "humanities" as an integrative study of man, of man's problems and man's achievements. These relate to the concepts of the previous chapter; the problems are analogous to the unanswered questions, and the achievements are analogous to the answers that have been given to the questions throughout the story of mankind.

In the Renaissance are found several characteristics of the humanities that were then revolutionary, but that have persisted into our contemporary world. These characteristics provide a gestalt for the teaching of humanities. The characteristics can, very broadly, be identified as *anthropocentrism*; a sense of human *continuity*; an appreciation of *versatility*; wide-ranging *inquisitiveness*; and a demand that learning have immediate *relevancy*. The five characteristics cannot be separated, for they exist together, in spite of seeming contradictions among them. Continuity, for example, requires an appreciation for the past, and this seems opposed to immediate relevance. Versatility, which implies an interdisciplinary approach, appears opposed to the unified concept of anthropocentrism; and persistent inquisitiveness calls all of the other values into question. There is, therefore, no best place to begin to discuss the five characteristics, and so, like any good humanist in doubt, I'll take the chronological approach.

Which presents a problem, for historians are in no agreement on where to begin the Renaissance. The eighth-century flowering of Charlemagne's court was a renaissance, but it was short and church-oriented and feudalistic in character. Peter Abelard's educational reforms—rational disputation rather than unthinking memorization—in the early twelfth century anticipate free inquiry and practical relevancy, but the issues he presents for debate in *Sic et non* are strictly doctrinal, despite the humanistic character of such questions as "whether it is permitted to lie, or not." Not so lightly disposed of is the ascension of learning in the thirteenth century, which saw the rise of the great universities at Paris, Bologna, and Oxford, where inquiring scholars developed more or less systematized institutional islands of resistance to rigid reliance on established views. There Aristotle was rediscovered, and with him came a need for Aquinas's rational, though dogmatic, apologia for the medieval church. There, too, began Roger Bacon's proto-science; and Albertus Magnus—the Doctor Universalis—ended intellectual isolationism when he brought Arabic, Jewish, Neoplatonic, and Aristotelian elements to bear on matters of botany and archaeology. And by the fourteenth century, Dante, Petrarch, Boccaccio, and, later, Chaucer had found beauty and immediacy in the vulgar tongues. Petrarch, in particular, is a Renaissance figure, for, in addition to using the modern Italian language, he took an entirely new view of Latin, considering it not only a language to be used for dialectical exercises, but one to be read for beauty and literary value. In this respect, Petrarch (1304-1374) may be the first humanist.

Humanism, in its most restricted sense, was a scholarly movement that revived great works of the past, restored literary studies, and, in so doing, rediscovered man-made beauty; but it slid rapidly into pedantry. Humanists per se fretted about grammar, analyzed calligraphy, collated texts, disputed about literary analogues. Their humanism had all the vibrancy, immediacy, and beauty of the French Academy, which, I have learned, recently debated whether or not *white* may or may not be defined in reference to the color of milk and snow (milk was stricken; snow retained). But humanists per se did more than this; they scrounged about in dusty, moldering monastic libraries, searching for forgotten classical manuscripts. Among the scroungers was one Poggio Bracciolini, a Florentine, who, while attending the Council of Constance in 1416, discovered in the nearby monastery of St. Gall a complete text of Quintilian's *The Training of an Orator*. With this, real humanities was born, for by 1428, a mere dozen years later, the Italians had replaced the old medieval trivium and quadrivium with a new curriculum, the humanities. The revolution is not startling on the surface, for it is marked mainly by the addition to the Florentine faculty of chairs of moral philosophy and rhetoric. But what it really means is the study of the classics for practical application to life—relevance to man rather than support of established views—and the study of the classics for beauty and style. Couple with this Quintilian's student-centered approach—he taught with respect for individual differences—and you can see the antecedents of the modern humanities movement. One of Poggio's contemporaries, Leonardo Bruni of Arezzo, is apparently to be credited with naming the humanities. "*Litterae humanae* are so called because they bring our humanity to completeness," he wrote; and he said, too, that "the liberal arts owe their name to the fact that they liberate man and make him master of himself in a free world of free spirits."

Midway between Poggio's discovery of the complete Quintilian and the new university curriculum was the importation by Giovanni Aurispa in 1423 of 238 Greek manuscripts that introduced modern-age Europe in one grand moment to the *Iliad*, the *Odyssey*, the works of Aeschylus, Sophocles, Euripides, Aristophanes, Pindar, Theocritus, Herodotus, Thucydides, Xenophon, Demosthenes, Ptolemy, Strabo, and the dialogues of Plato! The effect of the discovery of ancient Greece upon Western Europe and upon its very concept of man, is immeasurable. To conceive of modern man devoid of the Greek heritage is almost an impossibility; you have only to conceive Italy without tomato sauce, The Netherlands without chocolate, Germany without potatoes, or Spain without beans and pimentoes, to conjure up a sense-image of what a revolution in taste the Renaissance was. The variety in cuisine that followed the discoveries of Columbus can also be compared to the varied and versatile concept of man-thinking-and-acting that grew out of the discovery of the Brave Old World of the Greeks, with their inquiring minds, their love of beauty, their varied literature, and their scientific attitude toward history and geography. Man became, as Bruni had said, "master of himself in a free world of free spirits," and his striving toward realizing his now apparently boundless potentialities produced the Renaissance man. To take one of the earliest examples of Renaissance man, consider Leon Battista Alberti. Alberti, whose life spans the years from 1404 to 1472, learned Latin at Padua, Greek at Bologna, wrote a Latin comedy that passed for years as an authentic Roman play; wrote love ballads and sonnets in Italian; taught himself music and became proficient at playing the organ; wrote a treatise on the art of painting in 1435; indulged in archaeology, once attempted to raise a Roman galley; wrote books on horse-breeding, cryptography, and the family; was an architect who reintroduced pilasters to facade design, in both structural and aesthetic versions; and, in a self-induced program to compensate for physical weakness, became a considerable athlete. This, then, is a Renaissance man, and this is where I return to the practical problem of preparing a humanities curriculum for today's schools; for all the versatility, variety, and youthful enthusiasm of the Renaissance, except when it reposes in a man of Alberti's genius, exerts a powerful centrifugal and disintegrative force on the curriculum.

Earlier, I proposed a casual definition of humanities as an integrative study of man, of man's problems and of man's achievements. The key term here is *integrative*. There are in American schools two traditional academic methods of integrating the study of man; first, offering *courses* that integrate materials from the various disciplines; second, offering *courses of study* that expose the student to the various disciplines per se, thereupon requiring some kind of integrative project or seminar.

The problem that develops out of the first method is the possibility of superficial eclecticism. The problem that develops out of the second method is administrative. *Eclecticism* is often a misunderstood term. It ideally implies educated selection from varied sources for the purpose of developing an integrated whole that incorporates all of the best. In practice, eclecticism in humanities courses frequently result in one's roaring up and down the centuries, skimming off choice morsels *passim*. That is, it produces thirty-week courses in Man, God, and the Universe—with pictures. On the other hand, the piecemeal exposure to the several disciplines in separate courses is disintegrative, and the possibility of preparing an effective integrating seminar is slim, given the usual poor viscosity in the flow of communication among the departments of English, history, social problems, art, and music, and given the additional problem of finding a teacher suited for such a task.

In either method of integrating a humanities course of study, the selection of the teacher is the major and essential task. The teacher must have an integrative mind, which may be the result of his academic training or of his own natural talents or, all too rarely, of both. His interests must be broad, not only as they are implied in his college transcript, but also as they are exhibited in his way of life. Many humanities majors are such only because they were too snobbish for sociology and too ill-disciplined for the more conventional major programs. A humanities degree is sometimes a cocktail party patina that scratches all too easily in the academic grind. Furthermore, breadth of interest and training is not always coupled with organizational ability, and any inter-disciplinary program is a slippery creature to hold onto, exasperatingly octopusian in its direction.

Octopus or not, a true humanities course must be interdisciplinary. If one limits the study of man and his problems and achievements to philosophical matters, the result is a philosophy course, not a humanities course. If one limits the study to literary achievements, it is a literature course, not a humanities course; and if one limits the study to social achievements, it is a history course. If one limits the study to Latin or Greek, it is a foreign language course. Moreover, merely lacing philosophy, literature, or history courses with a few slides and a warmed-over award-winning television documentary is not integration. Nevertheless, such practices are a step in the right direction and might very well be planned as an intermediate stage in moving toward the humanities. It has been said that if English teachers and history teachers did their jobs, humanities and interdis-ciplinary studies would never have been needed. Let me explain.

Ordinarily in history and literature courses teachers cluster ideas around some convention of the prevailing ethos, such as Romanticism or the Enlightenment. Such an ethos will evoke intellectual creations in various forms. Conse-quently, there are often close relationships among artists in the different creative fields. Thus, in American romanticism, the cult extended from the writers Bryant and Emerson to the painters Thomas Cole, Asher Durand, and Washington Allston. Although there can never be a one-to-one relationship between the arts, common themes and attitudes are always present, and exposure to one medium will reinforce the image in the other media. In a remarkable number of instances, too, artists worked in several media. William Blake, Dante Gabriel Rossetti, D. H. Lawrence, and E. E. Cummings, for example, were painters. Hector Berlioz, Richard Wagner, and Gian-Carlo Menotti were at times their own librettists. Francis Hopkinson and John Dowland were composers, and Thomas Jefferson was an architect. Even where the relationships are not necessarily so immediate, the juxtaposition of artistic products from different fields is valuable. For example, one can relate Alexander Pope to Thomas Rowlandson, Ludwig van Beethoven to Kaspar Friedrich, Carl Sandburg to Aaron Copland, to Walt Whitman to Mathew Brady. Frequently, too, artists select their themes from other artists. John Quidor painted scenes from Washington Irving. Gustave Doré illustrated the *Divine Comedy*. Deems Taylor composed music for *Through the Looking-Glass*, and Charles Ives illustrated Emerson, Thoreau, Hawthorne, and Alcott in a piano sonata. These and many other parallels and relationships can be profitably brought into the English or history classroom—if one can locate and afford the supplies and equipment needed for their presentation.

That brings up the final problem of a humanities course of study. It is expensive. Slides, both purchased and specially made, film strips, movies, and recordings for only one course can cost up to $2000 or even $5000, and the equipment for presenting them as well as a teacher's time expended in ordering and organizing the materials are additional costs. For this reason, a modest budget spent to enrich existing courses over several years' time might be a better starting plan than a full-blown humanities program.

Money isn't everything, though. A thousand slides and a Schwann-filled music library are no aids to education if the teacher is not able to use them. A salted mine is no more than a salted mine, and no student will strike intellectual pay dirt from the mere garnishment of a literary course with nonliterary sources. He must be taught to see and to hear closely and critically, and he must be taught by a teacher who himself sees and hears. The disciplines *are* disciplined. Those who are truly interdisciplinary must be proficient in more than one discipline and at least passably competent in all. An admittedly Botticelli-like quiz for teachers might help explain my point: Two paragraphs above some thirty-five persons and titles were mentioned. The percent of these names a teacher can identify provides a fairly adequate gauge of his knowledge, though a high score on the quiz may not tell the whole story, for the thirty-five names mentioned are rather immediate in time and space—they include no classical allusions, no oriental allusions—and almost everything mentioned dates from the eighteenth century or later. Nevertheless, if a teacher is not familiar at first hand with, say, thirty of these artists and works, he probably is not yet ready to teach a humanities course. And if he didn't catch the contemporary allusions to Schwann and Botticelli, he may not be the aesthetic swinger that he may have thought himself to be. Knowledge of these details will not make a humanities teacher, but lack of such knowledge can keep one from being a humanities teacher. In short, there is no undisciplined short cut to humanities.

All of the above, I'm afraid, has been rather negative. Suppose, however, that one has the teacher with an integrative and disciplined mind, a faculty to support him, and a generous budget. How does one organize the course?

There are three approaches to interdisciplinary humanities courses, any of which is good. These three approaches are *area studies*, *period studies*, and *problem studies*. In *area studies*, one is usually limited to American or British studies (or some region of these nations) because of the language barriers in other cultures. In *period studies*, one could specialize, for example, in Classics, or the Renaissance, or the Enlightenment. Here, since one ranges across many national borders, reading works in translation is not so provincial. Finally, in *problem studies*, the teacher selects one or more themes—religion, liberty, aesthetics, the image of man, for instance—and examines these throughout world history. In the final accounting, no matter which approach is used, it will be, to a degree, a combination of all three. Thus, American Studies is necessarily limited in time period—post A.D. 1500—and will probably be further limited in theme— for example, the frontier, or anti-intellectualism, or nationalism.

What I have said so far is primarily applicable to the single course—a quarter, a semester, or a year—and it makes no provision for a continuing and cumulative course of study. I cannot say that I feel very guilty about this, because there are not many schools at any level that have achieved a rational progression even within the traditional disciplines, which are considerably less complex. There are a number of problems, of which the most obvious is the fact that the integrative-minded humanist is a rare beast anywhere, and one or two leaders cannot legislate a working curriculum. One can say, "Be thou a humanist," but I doubt that it would do much good. And even if a school were blessed with four humanities teachers (who intended to stay on), it is almost too much to ask for cooperation and compromise among them. Furthermore, one must avoid panacea thinking, and a school or college would be doing a severe injustice to students if it arranged a total educational program in humanities, for this would undoubtedly lead to ignoring vocational education and slighting disciplined technical studies. One must always remember that one can't do everything.

Nevertheless, a well-wrought, cumulative course of study in the humanities is possible, and really desirable. It is only necessary to decide on one approach—area studies, period studies, or problem studies—and then to divide by the number of school years required. The problem studies approach is very likely the best to begin with, for two reasons. First, it could eliminate wrangling among teachers, since every one could get his piece of Plato and Shakespeare. Second, it would eliminate the time-lapse perspective of the maturing student. By this I mean that one would not be obliged to set aside American sources, for example, for freshmen (high school or college), never to be seen again. By using the problem studies approach, and, for example, dividing the curriculum into three themes—Man and the Family, Man and Society, and Man and Reality—one could use, respectively, Shakespeare's *King Lear, Coriolanus,* and *The Tempest*; Euripides' *Medea,* Plato's *Republic,* Ovid's *Metamorphoses*; the Book of Ruth, the Book of Exodus, the Book of Job; Picasso's *Acrobats,* Millet's *Man With a Hoe,* Warhol's *Marilyn Monroe.* Each of these works could be used in respect to all three themes (consider *The Tempest* and the *Metamorphoses,* in particular), but I have set them in the order in which correspondences seem to me clearest. The cumulative effect in good students would be truly mind-widening, and any teacher would be happy to have a student who wanted to argue from previous experience that Job is a work of Man and Society, not Man and Reality; or that *The Tempest* is a family matter.

The examples of sources that I have given in this chapter are rather sophisticated, but I shall suggest alternatives later. I have not suggested specific assignments and methods of presentation and teaching, and more of that later, too. What I am insisting on here is that the teacher must for himself take the trouble to develop a fairly firm intellectual base in traditional humanism, and he must not suppose that humanities is a panacea. Planning a humanities curriculum is a peck of troubles, but all the troubles are worthwhile. The ideal of humanities courses hardly needs defense. In every sense of the word, they are liberalizing for both the student and the teacher, who are freed from slavish specialization, from limited exposure to the literary products of culture, and from narrow cultural provincialism. Humanities courses can effectively enrich the student's academic experience more than any other kinds of courses, and although they are, because of the sophistication of the materials involved, best suited for the high ability student, the sweeping variety of the education experience is equally appealing to the less able student. Nonetheless, I still say the teacher should step, not rush, where the angels have feared to tread. Their fears have not been unfounded.

III
It All Depends:
Uses and Abuses of the
Interdisciplinary Method

Once I knew a professor of English who told me that he hadn't read *Huckleberry Finn* because it wasn't in his field. That kind of clinging to narrow specialization is the greatest barrier to the interdisciplinary approach.

To deny the interdisciplinary method—to say that Michelangelo or Freud or Einstein or Phidias or Rabelais or Charles Ives or Huckleberry Finn is not in one's field—is unthinkable for the humanist, because for him the fields are far-flung: They are sophisticated baroque formal fields; they are oriental gardens; they are English parks; they are fields of daisies, ash heaps, and middens; and, as with Thoreau's philosophical gate at Walden, which bore no sign forbidding admittance, they are not private fields for pedants, but fields that give leave for all to enter who will. Once through the gate, however, one is not in one field, but in a tanglewood of myriad times, terms, and arts, with occasional clear glimpses through the undisciplined welter onto the varied fields of the humanities. The humanist's moments of satisfaction and intellectual repose are found in these fleeting moments of clarity.

But suppose that the teacher already recognizes the value of roaming far afield of restricted disciplines. He must then avoid the abuse of skimming over the top of culture apropos of nothing in particular. A satirical instance of this is a little film, *God is Dog Spelled Backwards*, in which, at subliminal speed and with psychedelic effect, three thousand years of world art is flipped before your eyes in the course of four minutes, ending abruptly with the announcement that "You are now cultured." That's how some humanities courses are operated, except that instead of one film they employ sixteen sound tracks of music, an Encyclopaedia Britannica philosophical film, and two batteries of slides. This abuse of the interdisciplinary method is aptly labeled the shotgun approach. The teacher covers a large area, but he doesn't penetrate very deeply.

The ideal, clearly, is somewhere between these two poles of rigid non-use and shotgun abuse. The ideal is where the method of crossing between the traditional disciplines is used, but not abused. And the ideal is the most dynamic and thought-provoking method of teaching humanities. It is also the most disorderly and dissonant.

The American composer Charles Ives was one of the world's major innovators in the use of dissonance in music. In a characteristic American vein, part of Ives's chief youthful pleasures was standing midway between a concert band and a drum and bugle corps on the Fourth of July. Listen to what happens when you stand between two harmonious entities in, for example, the second movement of Ives's *Three Places in New England*, or his *Fourth of July*, and you will have in your mind the essence of the use and the essence of the abuse of the interdisciplinary method in humanistic study and teaching. When one crosses disciplines, things fit, but they don't fit in harmony. In the case of Ives, the emotional response is reinforced, but the more conventional and disciplined aesthetic is discordant and offensive. Discord, therefore, is inherent in the interdisciplinary method, but discord is not always to be apologized for.

Another abuse of the interdisciplinary method—one that affects secondary school teachers too often—is the result of a shaky knowledge of history and influences. Last year a student of mine wrote an analysis of Robert Browning's "Their Last Ride Together" as a motorcyclist's love song. There's some virtue in this, of course. In my opinion it's better, and more humanistic, than a scrupulously footnoted analysis plagiarized from *PMLA*, or similar scholarly journals. Even so, there is such a thing as total misinterpretation, and frequently teachers, particularly high school English teachers, foster misinterpretation in their eagerness to encourage students to think originally and creatively. In any kind of literature, interpretation must develop out of what is actually there in print, and it must take cognizance of the context in which it was written. It is certainly true that literature, or any art of quality, has universal meanings, and the love tensions of Browning's poem are surely applicable today. It may even be true that this poem could be profitably compared to "The Leader of the Pack," a popular teen-age lament of the mid-sixties; but, nevertheless, "Their Last Ride Together" is simply not a Yamaha serenade. For teachers, of course, the misinterpretations are not so blatant as my student's. More often they take a modified form in which interdisciplinary analogues are artificially imposed upon specific works. To illustrate: A while ago I was asked what art works should be used in conjunction with teaching *The Great Gatsby*. I couldn't think of anything from what is known as "serious" art. *Gatsby* seems to me to be a literary work, and it might be that the best thing would be to compare it with some other literary works of the period, or if the teacher feels a strong need to be interdisciplinary, to rifle the bins of popular culture—magazines and tabloids of the twenties, particularly the advertisements, John Held's cartoons, or maybe some of the more sophisticated silent movies of the

time. Some works are neither deeply nor immediately interdisciplinary, and for these the best course is to be profoundly
narrow rather than tenuously superficial. In my own classes,
for example, I will spend weeks at a time on strictly literary
or political or historical sources; and only rarely do I use
pictures to accompany poetry or music—a practice that is
sometimes valid, but most often is ludicrous.

Let me give an example that I once used in a talk to
humanities teachers. While reading the first stanza of Wordsworth's "I Wandered Lonely as a Cloud," I flashed on the
screen a picture of a cloud, a picture of daffodils (from a
Burpee's seed catalog), a picture of a lake (Lake Superior, as
a matter of fact), and a picture of some trees with flowers
growing beneath (Canadian dogwood under birches). How
much value, I asked, is to be gained from this kind of
interdisciplinary study? Even if one corrected the complete
distortion of landscape implied by using scenes of northern
Minnesota to evoke mental pictures of the English Lake
District, is this practice valid?

My question of how much is gained in this kind of
superficiality is not entirely rhetorical, and the answer to the
question, like so many questions in pedagogy, is: it depends.
It depends on the students, because even such bulbous
imagery as Burpee's provides may not be wholly irrelevant. If
the teacher is working in an urban ghetto, perhaps a flower
catalogue is an important tool in his teaching.

Of course, if a poet is a good poet and if his poem is a
good poem, his images have greater descriptive precision than
a micrometer, but one cannot understand the tenor of a
metaphor without some knowledge of the vehicle (a point on
which I will expand in a later chapter).

Consider Edgar Allen Poe's "To Helen":

> Helen, thy beauty is to me
>   Like those Nicean barks of yore,
> That gently, o'er a perfumed sea,
>   The weary, way-worn wanderer bore
>   to his own native shore.

On desperate seas long wont to roam,
Thy hyacinth hair, thy classic face,
Thy Naiad airs have brought me home
To the glory that was Greece,
And the grandeur that was Rome.

There are a number of difficult references in this poem, but since I already introduced the flower catalogue, let me examine the phrase "thy hyacinth hair." A teacher might try, as I have tried without success, to explain this image verbally; but he might more profitably present a picture of a classical statue, with its involuted and convoluted stylized hair, and thus help his students to see why it is that Helen's beauty brings to the poet "the glory that was Greece / And the grandeur that was Rome." Is that *use* or *abuse* of the interdisciplinary method? Does it obfuscate or illuminate? Is it profound or superficial? The answers to these questions are the same: it all depends on the students, the teacher, and the situation.

Allied to the abuse of the interdisciplinary method that stems from uncertain knowledge of history and influences is the abuse that results from inadequate knowledge of semantics and aesthetic terminology. One obvious example of this abuse is the confusion that arises from including in the same category of classical arts the classical architecture of the Maison Carrée at Nîmes and the "classical" music of, say, Richard Wagner. This is not right. Classical "A" is not classical "B." "A" connotes order, symmetry, and respose, while "B" connotes individuality and passion. To avoid the misinterpretations that linking "A" and "B" fosters, a teacher might start a discussion of, say, Neoclassical aesthetics by presenting, for example, some eighteenth-century English country music, the rococo painting of Jean Honoré Fragonard, and Thomas Gray's satire "Ode on the Death of a Favourite Cat, Drowned in a Tub of Gold Fishes." Here, works of art form three disciplines, but all in the same general period of time, reinforce one another, exemplifying different aspects of order, social satire, elegant artificiality, and sophisticated class consciousness.

A presentation such as this can serve as a center for informed discussion on historical, philosophical, and aesthetic matters. Many questions arise: Are the dates of production nearly the same? Does it matter? Is any distortion embodied in shifting from France to England? Is the eighteenth-century country dance to be placed on equal footing with the urbane art of Gray and Fragonard? Have other aspects of eighteenth-century aesthetics been ignored? Can ignoring these be defended? Are these three works trivial? Do they ignore class struggles? Or are they satirical? Are the artists socially irresponsible? How great is the social function of satire? Are there any absolute scales of value against which one can judge trivial works of art? Is there today any area of our society like that implied in these works of art? Were these works regarded as modern when they were first produced? In what way might they have been modern? Can one find modern significance in them today? Is pop art similar? And so on.

These questions point up once again the dissonance that is inherent in combining statements from different arts. The examples that I suggested fit together, it is true, but not so perfectly as to stifle discussion or dispute. The purpose of such a presentation is to promote thought, not to impose an interpretation, as I did when I provided one-for-one photographic images to accompany Wordsworth's lyric. If a teacher shows an aerial photograph of Finland while playing Sibelius's Second Symphony, or if he holds up a tootsie roll while playing Stan Getz's jazz piece of that name, or if he plays a piece by Palestrina while showing Flemish medieval stained-glass church windows, he will have planted an interpretation in his students' minds; and in each case, there will be danger of misinterpretation: Sibelius did not have an aerial view of Finland, and his music may not be landscape "painting" at all. "Tootsie Roll" may have significance merely as a sexual pun in the jazz title, and Getz's rendition of "Tootsie Roll" is hardly distinguishable from his "Hershey Bar." Palestrina was neither medieval nor Flemish. There is, though, nothing terribly wrong with any of these correspondences, if they are effective in winning a student's interest. The skill of listening to abstract music with ears opened and eyes closed is not a universal gift. However, the teacher who uses the "multisensory" presentation must impose restrictions on himself; he must always remain honestly conscious of what he is doing and why he is doing it. If his purpose is merely to hold the students' interest, well and good; but let him be honestly conscious of that purpose, and let him forswear using that interest for personal ends. Good humanities teachers are Pied Pipers who can lead the students anywhere, but they must keep themselves honest in their piping, for no one else will do it. The multisensory presentation can sometimes become an award-winning performance rather than teaching, can deteriorate into no more than glittering facility, a kind of cultural showing off. Whether the multisensory approach is a valid teaching device, or merely a means of ego satisfaction for the performer and thus an abuse of the interdisciplinary method, depends on whether or not the teacher really uses his examples.

In the classroom, this multisensory method might have some value as an introduction. It would probably have more value as a conclusion. And, with careful planning, it could be used brilliantly by individual students or small groups as a final project. That is, the teacher might suggest that the students select, say, three works from three disciplines that would exemplify the theme on which they had been working. The details must be left to the teacher and the students, but the old rule applies here, too.

It all depends.

It depends on the age, the sophistication, the social background of the students. For some, the project might yield Glenn Miller, zootsuits, and a Loose-Lips-Sink-Ships poster. For others, it might yield the "Battle Hymn of the Republic," *The Red Badge of Courage*, and Winslow Homer's *Prisoners at the Front*. Or Chaucer's "Prologue" to the *Canterbury Tales*, the Duc du Berry's *Book of Hours*, and the facade of Rheims Cathedral. What is chosen depends, too, as the examples above might suggest, on what kind of course the teacher is teaching. The multisensory approach is one of the most adaptable practices of humanities teaching. In the full-blown humanities course it is an essential method, regardless of what kind of organization has been selected for the course curriculum. In period studies, or the cultural epoch organization, it is the only way to evoke a totality in each period being investigated, and this is true in area studies and problem studies as well. And it also applies to the traditional disciplines. For several decades now, American college and high school textbooks in history, literature, and foreign languages have included illustrations of art and architecture, and these are becoming more common and more comprehensive. In most classrooms, however, these illustrations are neither used nor abused; they're simply unused. Therefore, the first and most elementary step in converting English, history, and language teachers into humanities is to win them to making full use of their basic textbooks. This is easy to say, but I know it is not easy to do, not only because of the possibility of stubbornness or cultural myopia, but because the teachers already possess one of the characteristics of the true humanist, which Nicholas of Cusa named *docta igno-rantia*, the conscious ignorance of the truly learned. Suggestions of ways to compensate for this ignorance are the subject of a later chapter, but, for the present, I would suggest that every teacher at least try to use the interdisciplinary materials in his textbooks. I would almost guarantee that three minutes of class time on a picture of the Pantheon this year will turn into fifteen minutes next year, with better informed questions, and just maybe some well informed answers.

Before I proceed about the uses of the interdisciplinary method, however, there are a few matters to clear up to avoid getting too bewildered in the tanglewood of intertwined disciplines. First of all, how is what I have set forth different from audiovisual aids? The difference, I think, is that "the medium is the message." That is, I am not interested in *aids* to education—although of course the physical presence of film and slide projectors and tape recorders is an acknowledgement of the need for audiovisual aids—but what I am advocating is the use of materials from different disciplines that exemplify human expression. The second matter has to do with the word *method*. To some scholars, the term *interdisciplinary method* means methods of scholarly investigation, as, for example, when one uses sociological content analysis along with literary criticism to investigate aspects of a given culture, or when one uses psychoanalytic methods in studying works of literature or historical personages. To such people, what I am suggesting may appear superficial and a bit cavalier.

But it isn't, because my interest here is in methods of presenting humanistic material to students in the classroom. To repeat, my subject is not aids to humanistic education, but the very content of humanistic education—with suggestions toward means of presenting that content. Another possible criticism is that I am guilty of popularization. My answer to that is you bet I am! That's what teaching is all about; and whenever old methods have ossified to the extent of making learning rigid and restrictive and unpopular, some attention-getting theatrics may be worth trying.

A final matter to be cleared up is that I've given no definition of the term *interdisciplinary*. This omission has been deliberate. When the humanities approach to teaching gets hung up on definitions, counter-definitions, and panel discussions on redefinitions, the death knell will have been rung on the life and the force of the humanities that have attracted teachers to this integrated way of viewing knowledge and experience. What the humanities embody is the human approach, the man-centered approach. In a time when students are objecting to traditionally narrow courses of study, humanist teachers can restore to human beings a creative force. They can show the students, and, I should hope, some of their colleagues that the world in which we live is not necessarily always compartmentalized and departmentalized, and that it is possible for the individual man and woman to create an integrated world from the diverse currents of events that impinge upon their lives. The humanistic approach allows teachers to give some guidance to the creation of individual mainstreams where the tributary courses can be regarded as contributing to whole life.

The abuses that I've discussed do not exhaust the possibilities. A quick review might be helpful, however. First narrow specialization—nonuse—is the greatest enemy of the interdisciplinary approach. Second abuse of the interdisciplinary method is shotgun superficiality. Third abuse is distorting of history. Fourth abuse is distorting aesthetic concepts. Fifth abuse is the award-winning performance. Very well, but how does one *use* the interdisciplinary method? There is no simple answer to this question, because the appropriateness of interdisciplinary teaching always depends upon the prior experiences of the students and upon the purpose of the class. Take this chapter as a case in point. If in this chapter some point has been made clearer or more thought-provoking because of specific references to art or music or poetry or flower catalogues, then I have properly used the method. Similarly, if teachers can make their students understand the Romantic revolution better by presenting and analyzing works of painting, music, and architecture as well as history and literature, or if they can make mythology humanistically man-centered by looking at the Orpheus legend in Ovid's poetry, Poussin's painting, Gluck's opera, and the Brazilian film *Black Orpheus*, they are using, not abusing, the interdisciplinary method of teaching.

Earlier, I exemplified the disharmony inherent in crossing disciplines, by myself crossing disciplines and alluding to music, sound, harmony, and dissonance. I said that the dissonance in the music of Charles Ives contained essences of the use and of the abuse of interdisciplinary methods. In the realm of acoustics, the point can be illustrated more essentially, that is, in simpler form. If one takes, for instance, a tone of 256 vibrations per second and one of 271.2 vibrations per second and plays both simultaneously, there is both dissonance and a reinforcement of waves at given points. The "discipline" of C is pure; the "discipline" of C-sharp is pure. Intertwine them and there results that which makes real humanities exciting—the reinforcement of essentials amidst discord.

IV
The Teacher as Bartender:
Socratic Discourse
and the Great Conversation

My father-in-law is a connoisseur of bartenders. He will, on occasion, stop in at a tavern, buy a drink merely as a ticket to the "show," and watch a skillful bartender catalyze conversation. The bartender, according to the traditional rules, is never a discussion leader, but neither is he a follower, because he owes first allegiance to the Institution, and if he were to become a follower he would become part of a faction, which would be destructive of his Institution (that is, the tavern), which thrives on tolerance of all factions and on independence from all factions. The bartender, because of his Institutional independence and tolerance, serves as arbiter, but his arbitration must never set one faction above another. No one must leave his bar with less confidence, less self-respect, or less sense of identity than he came in with. If anything, the patron must leave enlarged with greater confidence, self-respect, and sense of identity. Alcohol does part of the job, it is true, but probably its only function is that of reducing barriers to self-expression. It is the social atmosphere provided by the bartender that builds individual men and women out of mass beings. In addition to being a catalyst-guide and arbiter, the bartender is an advisor. When advice is wanted of him, he must give it, but it must never be given *ex cathedra*, for the continuance of the Institution depends upon a state in which ill-advised action will never come home to roost. Hence, the task of the skillful bartender requires that all patterns of action—all advice—be evoked from the patron, who may have sought the bartender as advisor, but who must actually make his own decisions and formulate his own advice. Finally, the bartender cannot make men in his own image. He must take men as they are, and allow them to develop their ego potentials as they wish, but only if they wish, for he must respect the desire for silence as much as the desire for communication. Disrespect has but two forms, for the bartender has only two police actions to perform: the suppression of abusive drunks and the ringing of the curfew.

For that aspect of humanities teaching whose goal is building self-respect and a sense of being a dignified human being within humanity, the bartender's skills are well worth emulating. A teacher who can, like the adroit bartender, provide an environment in which free self-expression produces self-realization and self-induced inner-direction, is most certainly a humanities teacher. If he is a teacher of students who possesses a poor self-image and a low sense of potential, this aspect of humanities is quite obviously paramount. Within this "culturally deprived" context, "Great Books" humanism is largely irrelevant, because for such students the initial problem is not a matter of feeling contemporary with Descartes, Sophocles, or Daumier; rather, it is a matter of feeling part of the immediate world, of joining the *now* part of the human race. In such a context, humanities teaching is only a vaguer adjunct of vocational training, where the purpose is to help the student with low potential to find a respectable place within the existing economic society. The vocational teacher helps the student answer the question

"What am I?"; the humanities teacher provides an environment for the student to ask and to find an answer to the question "Who am I?" The teacher, like the bartender, acts as sympathetic ear and tolerant catalyst.

What is humanistically significant about the talk in taverns and cocktail lounges? Betting on football games, exchanging ethnic jokes and sexual stories are hardly significant topics. However, a large amount of barroom conversation has to do with the apparently trivial question: "What happened to me today?" And within the answers to that question are all the questions of the humanities. Let me illustrate with some answers to the question of "what happened to me today" and the subsequent humanistic questions that result from the answers:

A. "I had a quarrel with my wife today."

Q. What is the nature of marriage? Are women's values different from men's? What is family love?

A. "My friend has been promoted to foreman, and he's acting different."

Q. "How much behavior is the result of role-playing? What is innate behavior? What is friendship? What is the relationship between an institution and the individuals within it? To what degree is personal character consistent?

A. "I watched 'Bonanza' last night. It was a good one."

Q. "What is entertainment? What is good entertainment? Is good entertainment good art? What is the line between entertainment and art?

A. "I see that we're in for another tax increase."

Q. How do major political and economic occurrences
affect people? What is the relationship between citizen and government? What is good government? What
does a citizen owe to his government?

In short, the events of the day, when they imply either
problems or value judgments, are grist for the humanist's
mill. And while all these questions are worthy of scholarly,
literate, educated answers, they can all be approached with
common sense, personal experience, and the immediate
environment as source tools. To reiterate my points: The
humanistic approach need not be aristocratic. It need not be
dependent on high literacy. It need not stress historical
sources. The teacher as bartender can utilize current events to
point out humanistic problems and meanings; he can develop
humanistic interdisciplinary arts in the realm of popular
culture. All well and good.

But there are limitations to teaching humanities entirely
from the viewpoint of personal experience, limitations to the
usefulness of the teacher's role as bartender. The contemporary culture flow is often too easy, too glib, too cliché-
ridden. Conversation about popular culture and directly
immediate problems is a good door to humanistic education,
and for some students, all teachers can strive for in the
schools is to help them to the door, hand out membership
cards in the human race, and wish Godspeed. But conversation about the immediate culture is no substitute for
formal learning, and it can easily deteriorate into barroom,
cocktail lounge, slumber party chitchat. The bartender
cannot convey this formal learning. Only the well educated
teacher can. Only the teacher can balance the relevance and
immediacy of present-day man and his problems with the
perspective gained from the great works and men of the past.
Relevance in the humanities is a two-way street, and the
backward-looking direction is full of signs, symbols, restrictions, side alleys, all labeled in different languages and foreign

colors. All these need explanation and interpretation. In a word, they require the formal education that only the teacher can provide.

The good humanities teacher must, then, recognize the points at which he ceases to be the sympathetic bartender and becomes the teacher. A short time ago, I observed a "humanities" class in which senior high school students foundered joyously through a year of slumber party gossip, all carefully designed to avoid learning. The teacher, I rather think, had been inoculated with "sensitivity training," and he had developed a classic case of overdose. The cocktail lounge atmosphere was augmented by lowered shades and jazzy background music. The teacher and students sat in a circle and talked about love and marriage. Like, I mean, man, free love, group marriages, and premarital blisses and kisses. This, of course, is all New, and irrelevant to John Gay, François Rabelais, Geoffrey Chaucer, Aristophanes, and other dirty old men of the past. The teacher-bartender guided the conversation with a feather-light hand, involving everyone in his own scrupulous non-environment. Example:

Bartender: Do you think sometimes your parents don't understand you?

Student: Sometimes they never listen when you try to explain why you want to stay out late.

(SILENCE)

Bartender: What about trial marriages?

Student: Well, I don't know, you know? You know what I mean? I mean, sometimes it might be good, you know. I mean, do you really *know* if you want to spend your whole life with someone? You know?

Another Student: Why do people get married? Animals don't.

Bartender: Anything else about trial marriages?

Same Student: I really *mean* it. *Why* do people pair up? No one else does. And don't give me this stuff about ordained in heaven. I believe in God and all that—but *why* do people fall in love?

Bartender: What do you think about group marriage?

Same Student: Where did it begin? *I want to know!* If people really evolved, they must have been more like animals. When did they start getting married? And why?

(SILENCE)

Bartender: Do you think group marriages are a good idea?

And so on.

My concern here is not with the content of this class, but with the method of the class. Let me analyze it objectively for both uses and abuses. First, the lowered lights and background music are largely inconsequential. Midwestern rural bars in the full light of day are quite as open and conducive to free conversation as any dimly lit, intimate downtown lounge. Anyway, high school students have always been able to discern the basketball backboards through the twisted crepe paper at prom time, and I'm sure that one could move the Bolshoi Ballet into a high school classroom, and students would still know where they were. Nevertheless, the out-of-placeness of the cocktail lounge effects may produce some dissonance in the student that will make him more ready for original discussion.

Sitting in a circle is decidedly more conducive to free exchange of opinions than traditional classroom seating. On the other hand, any teacher who thinks that the round table makes everyone equal has a pretty low opinion of his students' common sense. The teacher, like the bartender, may be as much of a buddy as he wishes, but the teacher, like the bartender, runs the cash register and the curfew bell, and no customer or student ever got confused about the difference—and that difference makes all the difference. Young teachers of high school and college students are more susceptible to the "equality fallacy" than are elementary school teachers, who are not so naive as to suppose that the children cannot tell that *some*one in the classroom is one foot taller, epochs older, and in possession of the answer key. Which brings me to a more significant point. Everyone knows the old story of the first-grader who tells his parents, "My teacher sure is dumb; she keeps asking us questions." The story is a joke, because everyone knows that the first-grade teacher doesn't ask questions because she wants the answer; she asks questions to evoke correct or thoughtful responses from the children. This is not, however, true with all questions. When, for example, the elementary school teacher asks, "Which song did you like best?" or "How did you mix that color of paint?" the child is the authority, not the teacher. In like manner, the humanities teacher, who is so deeply involved in questions, which are, in one sense, the very content of his course, must clearly differentiate in his own mind which are legitimate Socratic questions—which are questions about which the student is authority—and which are "teaching" questions. The distinctions between these kinds of questions are worth drawing with some care.

The major distinction is that between questions which are patently answerable and those which are unanswerable, at least in an empirical sense. The latter group includes subjective questions of taste and ethics, as well as cosmic questions. This distinction is of the utmost importance, because, as in the class conversation I repeated above, the teacher's inability to make the distinction causes his excellent rapport with his students and his undirected discussion to become a travesty of humanistic education. The teacher's (bartender's) questions were well designed, nonanswerable (subjective) questions, whose purpose was partly to build self-confidence—an unnecessary purpose, since the class was entirely composed of moderately wealthy scions of well educated houses. But I felt sure that the questions had a second purpose, to evoke meaningful, relevant questions from the students; and yet the teacher stubbornly, or ignorantly, refused to recognize what I regarded as the total success of his method: the student's question of how marriage, as an institution, began. There may be no answer to this question thus far, and it may be an ultimately unanswerable question, but in spite of this, it is a highly legitimate question. It is a question for a true humanist scholar.

There was no need for the teacher to have leaped in with both Establishment feet to deliver himself of a lecture on anthropology, mythology, zoology, biology, animal and human psychology, along with illustrations from art and literature, ancient and modern. He could have continued in the bartender mode, asking such questions as: Does the question merit answering? Where might one look for answers?

Eventually, however, if the teacher is a teacher, he must cease to be coy. He can't play dumb forever. He knows, presumably, that there is such a thing as *The Readers' Guide to Periodical Literature*, the *Social Science and Humanities Index*, *Psychological Abstracts*, the library card catalogue, the Dewey Decimal System, bibliographical listings in encyclopedias; and he should tell his students about them. Even if he could draw the Dewey Decimal System out of students by elaborate questions, why should he bother? Why does he not tell them about it? It is all very well to know that, potentially, we could all discover fire, speech, the New World, printing, and Antarctica ourselves, but since all these things have been done, it is ridiculously time-consuming, it is dishonest, and it is degrading to make believe that the teacher doesn't know about the achievements of man.

However, the teacher cannot supply answers to every question his students ask, and therefore it is extremely important that he listen keenly to all his students' questions (sitting in a circle may *symbolize* respect for the students; listening to them will *realize* it) and that he recognize when a question has moved from conversation to discussion and from discussion to investigation—three very different realms.

Conversation is an art whose end is pleasure, self-satisfaction. It is the art of the successful party. It is the most humanizing of purely social arts. It can be stimulating, and it should be democratic. No one wins a conversation, because there is no contest. There are but two parts to conversation, illustration and dispute, and dispute is only the catalyst for further illustration. The illustrations of conversation are spontaneous, and, consequently, they are derived from personal experience, and that is why conversation is humanizing. What happened to me today matters, and I matter in a conversation. In conversation, one may talk about a problem, or an issue, or an object, but the real subjects of conversation are totally subjective—they are the conversationalists themselves. In good conversation one's personality, one's identity, develops; in great conversation, everyone's identity develops. Conversation restoreth the soul, which is why coffee breaks and cocktail hours and unstructured parties exist. Here is where we severally say, I'm me and I matter.

Conversation moves about its topics; discussion moves toward a subject. Within a schoolroom, conversation must convert to discussion, because the purpose of a school, anywhere, is not solely refreshment and restoration of the soul. In conversation, the medium is the message; that is, content is not paramount in conversation. The real subjects are the identities of the conversationalists. In the class that I observed, the teacher deliberately and perversely bypassed the transition point when the student presented a subject for discussion and investigation. This is extremely odd, since the teacher wished to have undirected, student-centered interchange of thoughts and experiences, and yet, in his eagerness to avoid a hard-and-fast subject for everyone, he insisted on his own topics for conversation. It is, of course, entirely possible that the student's question was not important or interesting to all of the class. But some questions have to be singled out for extended discussion. My own tendency is to be rather authoritarian and to have the entire class work on a project that looks worthwhile to me, although it is also possible to use the undirected conversation as a base from which to "peel off" individual students and smaller groups to a variety of subjects for investigation.

For example, the teacher might have stopped the general flow as soon as he recognized that a possible discussion question had developed out of the free interchange. He might thereupon have switched to highly structured discussion, using a method that was recommended by one of the participants in a workshop I conducted on teaching humanities. This teacher, recognizing that discussion aims toward a subject, with the ultimate goal of a decision or statement about the subject, maintained that unless the discussants are highly experienced in group decision-making, some external pressures are needed to force attention to the subject and to force a decision. Adopting this method, and using arbitrarily determined standards of, say, six discussants with a six-minute time limitation, the teacher in the round table discussion might well have divided his class into groups of six and given them six minutes to determine whether or not the question of the origin of the institution of marriage seemed worth pursuing. This procedure seems trivial, and yet it is an essential problem in the orderly discussion of any problem, be it moral, ethical, political, religious, philosophical, or aesthetic: Does the problem warrant further action? Or, put another way, the first problem is to determine the relevancy or irrelevancy of the proposed subject. At this point, if the teacher continues to ·wish to avoid imposing a subject on his students, he can divide the group into those who want to continue, and those who do not. The latter group may return to general conversation, while the former must continue with structured discussions of such six-minute subjects as: What is the precise nature of the question? How is the subject to be investigated? What kinds of information are lacking? Where might they be found? What might be the most efficient means of dividing labor?

Once a subject for investigation is chosen, the teacher should function as a source of information, not only for facts, but for techniques of investigation, which may in some cases become a major lesson. For example, a problem may require that the student develop full knowledge of library reference tools, or familiarity with detailed sources in a specialized discipline, or extensive personal interviews. The teacher may choose to supervise closely, with outside experts, tours, and practice exercises, or he may limit his participation to acting as a bibliographical source, but he must not neglect his informational function out of an attitude of misplaced coyness. Pretended ignorance on the part of the teacher is dishonest, it is a disservice to the student, and above all, it is an insult to the intelligence and self-respect of the student. While it is important that the humanities teacher not dictate decisions of taste, morals, and policy, it is equally important that his admitted ignorance about right answers to moot questions not be extended to a pose of stupidity. What's the use of a teacher growing older and submitting himself to formal education if he is going to deny knowing more than his students? It is one thing to deny having achieved wisdom by the age of fifty, but it is quite another thing to deny having learned anything at all by the age of fifty. It is quite proper for a teacher to say that he does not (yet) know answers to the questions of *what is man, what is beauty, what is virtue, what is God*, but it is inexcusable for him to say falsely that he does not know the answers to the questions: *who was Socrates, what did he say, where can I find his words, what does this passage mean*? The bartender can be stupid, but the teacher must not be ignorant.

This brings me to the other two parts of the title of this chapter: "Socratic Discourse and the Great Conversation." Any humanities teacher, regardless of whether he is a teacher of ghetto teen-agers or of well-to-do college seniors, must be familiar with the Socratic method, and he must be familiar with the Socratic method firsthand as it appears in the *Dialogues* of Plato, because insofar as a humanities course is a course of questions, it is Socratic.

One of the most attractive of Plato's dialogues is *The Symposium*, which has given us the modern term. Histori- cally, a symposium was a "drinking together," that is, an after-dinner drinking party, which, incidentally, gives classical sanction to my analysis of teacher as bartender. The original *Symposium*, like the "symposium" that I described earlier, was a discussion of the subject of love. Unlike the high school symposium, however, it moved consciously from conversa- tion to discussion. The first few pages of the dialogue are purely conversational: remarks are exchanged about the host's (Agathon's) new play and about the hangovers that afflict the guests, who had been celebrating the first prize Agathon's play had won. Hangovers being what they are, the guests agree not to drink, and the symposium ceases to have the character of a cocktail lounge; even the mood music is dispensed with—the flute player is sent away. The subject for discussion is rather arbitrarily selected by one Eryximachus, a physician, who has recently been conversing with his friend

Phaedrus about the lack of hymns to love. A roughly formal plan for taking part in the discussion is set, with Phaedrus speaking first, and then each man in the circle.

I shall not rehearse or analyze the points made about love—like students giving an "oral book report." There are, however, some relevant points about the method to be noted. First, conversation is clearly distinguished from discussion, and when discussion begins, the subject is stated, and the mode of participation is structured. Second, the participants support their stands both from personal experience and from literary and traditional sources. The discussion is quite interdisciplinary, for supporting arguments are drawn from myth, history, medicine, and poetry. Of particular significance is the fact that these two characteristics are true of Socrates' portion of the dialogue. Socrates, in other words, does not try to draw blood from a turnip. Socrates uses questions as a means of discovering truth, and Socrates uses a pose of ignorance as a means of eliciting participation in the search for truth, but Socrates assumes some degree of cultural experience among the participants, and also, as should be true of the teacher in the humanities classroom, Socrates knows what direction things are taking. The many "either-or" preliminary questions that Socrates employs are not haphazardly asked. Socrates knows where they are going, and, indeed, Socrates (as he appears in the *Dialogues*, that is, as partly a creation in Plato's image) has made up his mind ahead of time, and is using the questions as a means of involving his companions in humanity. If he makes them think, therefore they will be.

In that respect, reading and participating in the original *Symposium* is true humanities. It is the act of becoming part of what Mortimer Adler's Great Books movement called the "Great Conversation." In this participation, every man becomes contemporary with all mankind. The conversation and discussion that began in the fifth century B.C. is not yet over, and all may enter into it who will, for there is no sign to forbid admittance. The ticket to participation in the Great Conversation is the membership card in the human race. Its certification reads: I think, therefore I am—and I that am matter in mankind.

A final word: the *Symposium* ends its discussion of love with the entrance of the Athenian general Alcibiades, who is hilariously, roaring, maudlin drunk. The interchange of words for the purpose of examining a problem is lost in a welter of personalities and anecdotes and emotions. The flute player returns, drinks are poured. Discussion has ended—something which must happen in the schoolroom too—and conversation has returned to restore the souls.

V
How Not To Assign
"What-Did-You-Do-Last-Summer":
Creativity and Self-Expression
in the Humanities Classroom

Becoming human is not simply a matter of discussion, or of acquiring the cool-headed intellectual skill of analysis and synthesis of great art works. At some points in our lives we must become creators and producers of some things that are uniquely our own, some things that are self-expressive and, to a degree, *summae* of what matters most to us. Conversation and discussion serve as a step toward summary self-expression, but these are public social acts, impermanent and formless. Sitting in an audience or class is another vital step in becoming a human being, for we need to be receptors of the culture in which we live if we are to view ourselves in perspective, and therefore we need lectures, classes, readings, performances, and role-playing to provide condensed patterns for viewing our own experiences, as well as to provide condensed patterns for viewing our own experiences, as well as to provide a fund of secondhand experiences as touchstones for comparison. Nonetheless, to exist only as a receptor and interpreter is to be only half a human being. Fulfillment of the other part of being human requires

creative self-expression, which seems to be a basic human
need that will be achieved in one form or another. For
instance, on a cliff side not far from my home on the shore
of Lake Superior is the outline of a heart, and within the
heart is the message "Deb & Cam." This is a sample of
creative self-expression of a conventional sort, but honest
enough. It defaces the rock and the landscape; yet, within the
limits of the genre, it is rather appealing, because it is neatly
executed, the sentiment is boldly and clearly stated, and the
message emphatically announces that man, who thinks he
matters, has been here. My observations may seem over-
stated, but when we consider what Wallace Stevens made of a
jar in Tennessee, it is clear that small art is not beneath a
humanist. Wallace Stevens, in "Anecdote of the Jar," says of
the jar:

It took dominion everywhere.

The jar was gray and bare.

It did not give of bird or bush,

Like nothing else in Tennessee.

Art fixes experience, sets nature, takes dominion. Like
Neil Armstrong's rigidly extended American flag on the
windless moon, man's self-expressive creations are artificial,
and rarely do they blend into the landscape, or take dominion harmoniously. If this is so, why should we attack Deb &
Cam, but not Neil Armstrong and Wallace Stevens? I am not
excusing Cam's defacement of the landscape, nor am I calling
Wallace Stevens and Neil Armstrong litterbugs, but I am
asking, does all creative self-expression merit public display?
Further, if all self-expression does not deserve an audience,
why should anyone bother expressing himself?

These are debatable questions, but I suggest that the case of "Deb & Cam" may demonstrate that all personal expression does not deserve public display. Creative expressive forms for the community probably need to express some community values rather than, or in addition to, purely personal values. As to the question of why one should bother with self-expression if one isn't given license for public display, the answer is humanistic and existential: To become human is *to become*, and the creative act is a microcosm of the act of becoming. That is one justification for using creative projects in humanities programs, to help each student to develop and to express the uniqueness of his own humanity.

There is a second rationale for using creative activities, however, one which is closer to the traditional ideas of the humanities, and it is that creative projects promote understanding of artists and, thus, of their works. Students who complain of the "irrelevance" of *The Scarlet Letter* and *Paradise Lost* are complaining not only that the great works seem unrelated to contemporary news bulletins, but that they are not related to them personally. There is no single solution to this problem, but if the teacher can help the student relate himself to the creative act, every human creation will be potentially relevant to him. His relationship may be concern with the process of creation or with the artist's motive for self-expression, but, either way, his concern can grow out of the common human experience of the act of creation. Without this experience, his relationship with art and thought will be academic, and he will dutifully parrot the statement that Hawthorne wrote because he reacted against the Calvinist tradition, or that Wordsworth's writings responded to the Industrial Revolution, or that Aristophanes wrote as a critic of Socrates. All of these are valid enough views, and important, too, because Calvinism, industrialism, and Platonism are still with us today in modified forms, and

they are still relevant to contemporary men as sources of
inspiration or offense; but the process of arriving at the
relevant elements in these isms is both extended and intellectual, or, from the student's viewpoint, tedious and academic.
Understanding the human act of creation can provide a more
immediate bond between student and artist.

The initial creative experience for a student need not be
extended or profound. For instance, a composer I have met
has started his humanities students in music by having them
write a "score" for pencil tapping, in their own notation
system. A sculptor gives gobs of Plasticine to his humanities
students to experiment with. A writer distributes a random
collection of words to students to be arranged into a
"poem." Each of these practices is an exercise in creativity
and presents problems that confront any creator—problems
of form, content, purpose, limitations, choice—but all the
problems are presented without the usual demands of technical competence in reading music, drawing pictures, or spelling
and metrics. It is, of course, a giant step from an exercise in
pencil tapping to Beethoven's working of a shepherd's melody into the final movement of the Pastoral Symphony. It is a
giant step from casually worrying a lump of clay, to Michelangelo's envisioning the figures within a block of marble. It is
a giant step from rearranging words into an idle pattern to
Shakespeare's infusing life into an abbreviated chronicle of
barbaric history. But in essence the human act is the same,
and at least the students' microcosmic bafflement puts them
in pygmy step with the giants.

Beyond presenting introductory experiences in the creative act, the humanities teacher is restricted only by the time
available for further projects and by the limitations imposed
by the age of his students and his own creative talents. These
are significant restrictions, and for that reason the activities
that I will be suggesting are limited to writing and photography, neither of which calls for the specialized talents,

training, and equipment of music, painting, and the theater. Writing, of course, requires basic skills that may have been achieved unequally, yet those skills are the backbone of all formal education. Photography requires equipment, but, at least at the level of the snapshot, it demands fewer preliminary technical skills than the other arts. These statements should not be construed as meaning that I have selected what I regard as infantile forms of expression or that these are the best forms for every classroom situation. The practices I suggest are elementary, but the issues involved are not, and they can be adapted to any age level.

But before proceeding to more specific remarks about projects in personal expression, I have a word of caution regarding the degree of the teacher's involvement in his students' creative work and his guidance of that work into appropriate classroom channels. Ultimately, self-expression is the student's affair, and if he displays reticence about parading his inner lives, loves, and dreams before his peers and critics at the drop of an assignment, his reticence should be respected. Furthermore, while the humanities teacher is quite right in providing a climate for individual self-expression by means of making assignments that invite his students to bring forth their personal beliefs and experiences, the extent to which this purpose is part of the course must depend on the structure and the primary purpose of the course. If the main thrust of the course is joining in on the "great conversation" about great books, the self-expressive contributions of the students ought to be limited to incidental illustrations in discussion. If the teacher is primarily a historian and he feels uneasy about expressive projects, the activities might be best kept to the more objective interdisciplinary activities, such as slide-tape projects. If the humanities program is a team project with discrete classes in art and English, quite carefully planned projects in creative self-expression are possible, and they might serve as the inte-

grating act that makes this project a true humanities program.
But regardless of where the project in creative self-expression
is incorporated, it must not be haphazardly left to the
student's discretion.

A humanities project that has applications in many
classes and media is the personal narrative assignment used as
a creative exercise through which students can discover
themselves and their places in the greater picture of humanity
and the humanities. Whether the personal narrative approach
is used in classes in writing, history, art, or humanities, many
of the problems and techniques are interchangeable. The first
problem for the teacher is to make a concrete and workable
assignment, not simply a vague "what-did-you-do-last-summer" assignment of the kind that the students are assigned
every year and respond to with the same clichés and standard
stories each year. Cliché responses are not true expressions of
the *self*. They are expressions of the mass being.

The cliché story will not be the only bad result of vague
personal experience assignments. An allied response is the
ritual autobiography that presumes that conventional high
points (graduations, prize winnings, "big" games, making the
team) are important and interesting subjects for narratives.
They aren't. Such accounts would be better presented in lists
on an application form or in a high school annual or in a
family Bible.

If the personal story is to have any value to the student
beyond "practice," it must be designed to teach intellectual
skills. One of those skills, the skill of thoughtful and honest
introspection, is allied to interpreting literature. Related to
introspection is the humanistic skill of recognizing the really
significant occurrences in one's life that produce some basic
alteration in world view or identity. In other words, the
student should be trained to look for and recognize the
Joycean epiphanies of his life rather than to ascribe undue
importance to formal rituals. Weddings are important as

ritual, but understanding one's place as a peripheral "member of the wedding" can be more significant in a personal narrative.

How can teachers help students to find these moments of membership? One answer is to train them to look at moments, to freeze time. This is a skill possessed by some portrait artists, and it is a rare skill. It is also a skill possessed by cameras. Snapshots, therefore, can provide a student with a means of looking at himself and his experience objectively. Extrapolating a narrative from pictures is an action familiar to the student through his exposure to the frequent use of the device of stop action in movies and television, and the student will recognize that a still photograph is but one frame in a continuous narrative. Thus, as the student examines the picture that is to trigger his narrative, he should decide whether it is the beginning, the middle, or the end of the story, and the pictures must be regarded as objectively as possible: Who is this person? What can I learn of him from the objects in the background, from his clothing, from his expression? What is he doing? What are his motives? Is he acting a role, or is this really he? These are all legitimate questions, but the student should not be urged to jump to the interpretations until he has documented the evidence of what is there. Careful documentation is a technical skill of scholarship that often is glossed over in freewheeling humanities classes where books are discussed without reference to the author's printed words, and pictures are categorized without attention to what is on the canvas. Oddly enough, the disciplined technique of close observation of visual documents should not be new to any American, for we all learned it in kindergarten, but, to paraphrase E. E. Cummings, "down we forget as up we grow." Let me explain.

If you have ever watched a primary school child reading his "Run, Dick, run" book, you may have noticed how long the child lingers on each page. He does this because he is reading the page. All of it. The primary grade teacher spends considerable time teaching children how to read pictures for narrative content, and the pictures in the primers are carefully designed to provide a rich context for the little sentences and exclamations that adults love to scorn. Unfortunately, the talent for picture reading is allowed to atrophy throughout the elementary grades and is virtually dead by the time the student reaches high school. The problem for the teacher, therefore, is one of revitalizing old skills, not developing new ones. There are a number of methods of revitalizing picture reading skills. One method is for the teacher to spend a whole hour on a single picture, asking the students to identify everything in a painting, but not permitting any conclusions without identification of the evidence. Thus, when a student says that he sees "an old man," he should be made to recognize that this is a conclusion based on what he sees first—a man with gray hair and deeply lined skin. Another technique is to superimpose a grid of one-inch squares over a picture and list what is in each square. A third method for "reading" the details of pictures is one that I use in art galleries, and could be adapted to a classroom: I look through the viewfinder of my close-up camera, which is surprisingly rewarding, even with Jackson Pollock. These techniques are not ends in themselves, of course, but only exercises in close observation, and the value of objective observation to writing personal narratives is boundless, for it forces one to deal with what is there and not to squeeze one's own life into a Robert Hall ready-to-wear cliché. We are unique because of the succession of immediate environments in which we move.

Single snapshots, however, will not in themselves provide such a succession. For this, one needs a series of pictures, which can be viewed as a "career." In social-psychological terms, a career is the series of experiences and activities in a given role. Since any person occupies a number of roles, he will have an equivalent number of careers, some formal and regularized, as in the career of president of the senior class, and some informal. Informal careers that students have had could include the career of soap-box derby builder, of dish-dryer, of trout-fly tier, of horse story reader, of AM radio listener, and so on. The examples are trivial, but they will help the student to limit his topic and consequently to employ greater detail in his writing, and to compel him to write a truly personal narrative, one for which there is no conventional plotty pattern. And the careers need not be trivial: there are careers of activist, of poet, of artist, of career chooser—any of which could lead to deep and intelligent self-examination as well as to a sense of continuity in identity. I would encourage practice with the more trivial careers first, because with them it is easier for the writer to be objective and to regard himself from a less intimate vantage point.

So far what I have said about personal expression has required a considerable degree of literacy, at least minimal ability in penmanship, spelling, and sentence structure; and in that respect the narrative may be a discouraging project for some students. But thanks to films and cameras, creative self-expression is not tied exclusively to writing ability. With a camera of almost any quality, the photo essay or movie is a possibility, but, in many ways, it is no less demanding than a written narrative. If the project is a photo essay (that is, a collection of still photographs) to be made of past experiences, it requires selection, organization, and interpretation. Moreover, it requires a backlog of photographs that are not always available. Film expression of current existence can be an appropriate project, but it requires even greater objectivity of viewpoint than a written narrative that is based upon past experiences: it is much harder to select the significant occurrences of today than it is to select the significant occurrences of the past decades. In addition to this, the mechanical problem of camera self-portraiture almost de-

mands a team effort—that is, one cannot make a film
autobiography of a day in his life without a cameraman. One
can, though, use the camera to express his view of the world,
in either still or motion picture photography.

The arts of still photography and of cinema are not the
same, but, for a variety of reasons, still camera work provides
a valuable training ground for movie camera techniques, not
to mention the mundane fact that it is less expensive and
thus more feasible than filmmaking in many situations.
Because still photography does not confuse the eye with the
complexities of motion, students can be trained to take time
to look in all four corners of the viewfinder as well as at the
primary subject, and if they have had some experience in
analyzing the details in snapshots and in art works, they will
at least recognize the significance of background environment
in the total effect. A few unsuccessful camera experiences
will also inform the student of the limitations of the medium
in matters of exposure, distance, depth of field, light and
shadow, and shutter speed. That much is technical, as is
much more beyond the province of this book, but there is a
humanistic purpose here, for expressive forms must be
understood in the context of their technical limitations, and,
somewhere along the line, humanists should become aware of
this, at first hand. Amateur creative experiences with pen and
brush and piano are often abortive because of the limitations
of the amateur, whose inadequacies do not allow him to
approach the limits of the medium. The camera is more
democratic, and everyone can reach the technical limits of
the medium with his first experience of out of focus
overexposure.

More important to self-expression is that the camera's eye
shares the viewpoint of the human eye. In that respect the
value of a camera in personal expression is not that it
portrays the student as an actor in his life, but that it
portrays his life as he sees it. The eye of the camera therefore

requires that the student express himself not overtly, as subject-hero of his own drama, but truly as an artist-creator who is imposing an order upon the world. The ego in a personal film is implied rather than announced, and thus those in the audience are asked to share a viewpoint—a reasonable demand—rather than to honor an unfinished personality. This is the case whether the film moves or not. A dozen photographs that express the idea "this is a portion of the world as I see it" can be fully as eloquent as ten minutes of motion pictures; and the audience is free to expend more than ten minutes on them if the student's viewpoint engages them, and less than ten seconds if it does not.

The motion picture does, however, have great appeal to students, as well as built-in relevance, for whether we like it or not, we live in a McLuhan-land of moving plastic and electronic images. The problem in using the medium that teachers and students must deal with arises from their limited experience with movies. This may seem to be contradiction in McLuhan-land, but for most Americans, filmic experience is limited to viewing passively Hollywood extravaganzas and television series, neither of which provides appropriate patterns for a student's personal expression. In spite of this, many humanities teachers share the students' enthusiasm, and some are jumping on the moviemaking bandwagon with the same air of abandon and purposelessness that marks the teacher who assigns a personal experience essay on what-did-you-do-last-summer, and with much the same results of cliché responses—monster movies, spy adventure movies, and a welter of ill-composed shadows of Hollywood. These are delightful independent projects, but they hardly serve a humanistic end. I do not say that they have no educational value, for cliché stories, vague assignments, and junior G-man movies all provide technical "practice," and can develop facility of expression, which is important. But they should be indulged in with an honest admission by the teacher of this restricted purpose, if that is all he is aiming at.

It would be far better for the teacher to help students to see the possibilities in cinematic creative expression and to disengage them from cliché movies, with their astronomical budgets, studios, panoramic sweeps, professional actors, special effects laboratories, exotic settings, and heavy dependence on a synchronized sound track. As many teachers know, there are many short art films available that can provide more useful ideas for discussion of content and for close study of camera techniques and editing, and that provide suggestions for "no-budget" filming. Techniques that might be useful for student-made personal narratives include photographing a series of homemade drawings, using the immediate environment and amateur actors, and telling a simple story by silent editing. The effectiveness of the first technique can be demonstrated in such films as *Children's Dreams* (which animates children's paintings of their dreams), *Ballet by Degas* (which animates Degas's paintings), *A Trip with Currier and Ives* (which animates Currier and Ives prints). The use of the immediate environment is powerfully demonstrated by *The Jungle*, which is a film made by a teen-age gang in a black slum in North Philadelphia. And for silent picture story telling, Thomas Edison's film *The Great Train Robbery* is excellent both for film history and simple editing techniques. Another film that might provide useful ideas in stylized story telling is *The Loon's Necklace*, a Canadian Indian legend that was filmed in the forties, using traditional masks and painted backgrounds. All these are a far cry from what-did-you-do-last-summer, and they may hint at how far beyond stereotyped expressive forms students are capable of going, if teachers can show them the way.

The use of personal narrative and photographs and movies can be adapted to a variety of degrees of sophistication. In the secondary school humanities course it can be kept simple, with emphasis on the personality; for the college

student majoring in humanities it can be developed into a
senior project that makes use of many contributing courses.
For example, after taking several philosophy courses and
doing some college theater work, one of my students wrote a
trilogy of dramas exploring three concepts of the hereafter.
Another student produced a five-minute film that required
preliminary courses in design, filmmaking, music appreciation, and art history. In these cases, my emphasis shifted
from *personal* expression to techniques of arriving at *universal* expression. In other words, teachers can help students to
find means of expressing themselves that will bring them
beyond Deb & Cam's graffito, and closer to James Agee's and
Walker Evans's *Let Us Now Praise Famous Men*, where the
artist's eye and the camera's eye become our eyes, too.

Let teachers bear in mind, though, that their aim in
creative projects in a humanities class is not perfection of
execution, but honest expression, which implies clear-headed
introspection. When the time comes for teachers to ask for
self-expression, they cannot say of the student's project,
"This is wrong," when they really mean, "I wouldn't do it
that way." On the other hand, let teachers not excuse shoddy
execution or formless expressionism by labeling it "fresh"
and "creative."

"Creative self-expression" is a portmanteau phrase: almost anything can be stuffed into it, particularly in this day
of oblique and abstract expression. Abstract expressions,
however, are often an easy way out of the problems of
introspection, analysis, composition, of viewing oneself in a
larger human context—in short, of bringing order from
disorder, which is an unending human goal. The order that
artists, scientists, philosophers, and historians set forth may
be an uncovering of an ultimate cosmic order or it may be
the imposition of apparent form upon chaos, but in either
case, the search for order is one of the highest manifestations
of humanity. When we join in this quest, we become brothers

of Plato and the Buddha, of King Lear and Henry Adams, of Michelangelo and Darwin, of Don Quixote and Benjy Compson. Being a participant in this long quest demands not only summary statements, but a sense of becoming. Gods may spring fully clothed into mature existence, but we are not gods. We must become ourselves by passing through Shakespeare's Seven Ages, probably never to know what we will finally become.

VI
Getting Down to the Nitty and the Gritty of Teaching Literature: Metaphor, Myth and the Humanities

Every humanities teacher is in danger of leaning either too far in the direction of propriety or too far toward popularizing. Too much propriety will make humanities irrelevant; too much popularizing will make humanities pointless. Yet, on the one hand, humanities is rooted in the past and the finest achievements of mankind; and on the other hand, humanities is man-centered (student-centered) and immediate. Those teachers who overemphasize the past and other men's achievements produce dry, dehumanized, remote courses of irrelevancies; those who overemphasize the student produce courses whose banner seems to proclaim, "If you can't teach 'em, join 'em." Under this slogan, Sincerity, Participation, Expression, and Relevancy replace Knowledge, Precision, Craftsmanship, and Objectivity. All eight characteristics are virtuous, and, it must be clear, a balance among them would be ideal.

I am going to assume that most teachers are not like Miss Grundy, and that if they err, it will be in the direction of popularizing rather than proprietizing. And that is the reason that I want to get down to the nitty-gritty. The popularizer, in his desire to relate a work of art to his students, in his impatience to evoke sincere expression from them, and in his eagerness to promote meaningful discussion, will sometimes ignore the nitty-gritty of looking at the elements. In using art works, for example, such teachers will plunge into discussions of meanings before ascertaining what is on the canvas, as, for example, in the case of discussing the "sentimentality" of Grant Wood before examining what is actually in *American Gothic*.

In teaching about a given art form, a teacher never knows for sure how detailed the analysis should be. Superficial discussion without any attention to detail is bad, and leads to stereotyped opinions. Equally bad is analysis that passes the threshold of relevance. The threshold of relevance, of course, is a shifting point. Analyzing brush strokes in a late Titian may be relevant to a graduate student in art history, or to a student of oil painting, but it would be an irrelevant study for a student in a high school humanities course. The nuances of historiography are irrelevant to a student in an introductory course in world history. Problems of quartos and folios in Shakespeare studies are irrelevant to the high school student who is only trying to understand what Hamlet is saying. Chord progressions in Beethoven's Fourth Symphony are irrelevant to the student who is trying to hear the theme of the second violins amidst a welter of unfamiliar sounds. In each of these cases, the amount of detail depends on the students and the curricular context within which the teacher is working.

In some areas of study, the progressive order of relevant detail is traditionally well defined. Foreign language studies, mathematics, performance on a musical instrument, for example, have a pretty clear tradition of a progression of learning order from the simple to the complex. This applies to the physical and biological sciences as well as to most

Metaphor, Myth, and the Humanities

vocational studies. It is less true of the realms of social sciences and humanities, for here the teacher is never sure of the amount of ignorance he can presume to be the common lot of his students, because we all live as human beings, in an environment of social dynamics and cultural objects. This is particularly true of literary studies—"English," that is—for once reading has been mastered in elementary school, there seems to be no order in which literature is taught. In an almost pointless tradition that still dominates American schooling. The high school student is given a chronology of American literature, and then of English. Thus a student reads Edward Taylor before Longfellow, and Chaucer before A. E. Housman, and Whitman before Wordsworth, because that is what the national-chronological patterns dictate. It is all done as if there were no skills necessary to the reading of literature. It is done as if anyone could read anything with understanding. It is done as if it were true that anyone can teach literature.

There are good reasons for all humanities teachers to get down to the nitty-gritty of teaching literature. For one thing, the problems faced by English teachers in trying to develop a rational, cumulative pattern of study are shared by—and compounded in—the humanities. There is no accepted order of learning to be followed. Second, literature is the one discipline absolutely essential to a humanities course. Even when a course is developed around art, music, and film, it will not become a humanities course unless it deals with the literature of these arts. Lacking the literature, such a course must either become a vocational studio experience or a variety show with after-theater discussion. And I do not mean to limit the term "literature of the arts" to the secondary commentaries of history, criticism, and aesthetics. Understanding of much art work, for example, requires knowledge of classical and biblical literature, myths and folklore. Music has had perennial wedding to poetry from before Dryden and Purcell to after Simon and Garfunkel, and, like film, music has a close relationship to dramatic literature. Finally, the nitty-gritty of teaching literature relates to all the humanities, because the elements of the literary craft are frequently transferable to the other disciplines.

Now, let me get down to that nitty-gritty. I want to look at some elementary terms that are common to writer, critic, teacher, and student. The terms are not elementary in the sense of "Run, Puff, run," but they are elementary in the sense that nitrogen and hydrogen and magnesium and krypton are elementary. The elementary terms I've selected are *metaphor, image, symbol, myth, fable, parable,* and *allegory.* Some teachers might quarrel with this list, and some might be stung by the absence of a favorite literary term. To them I can only say that my choice was not haphazard and that I arrived at these terms by asking myself the hard questions: Which are elementary in that they are basic concepts from which other techniques can be developed? Which are elementary in the sense that they are simple first-things-first terms? Above all, which are most useful in contributing to finding relevance in literature?

The purpose of teaching literature always has been to establish some degree of relevance of literature to students' lives; but today, with the very legitimate demands of the students for even greater relevance, teachers must do all they can to distinguish between those technical aspects of literature which contribute directly to every student's understanding and those technical aspects whose relevance is important to a smaller number of students. The criterion to use in evaluating a technical device is the degree to which it contributes to the students' understanding of literary works.

Prosody, for example, is of small relevance to understanding. The techniques of meter and rhyme in a poem are largely irrelevant to the meaning of the poem. I am not saying that prosody does not matter, nor that prosody should not be taught. There is no question in my mind that all the technical devices of a good poem enhance the meaning. Female endings can enhance the feeling of repose in a meditative poem, and incidentally, are used to good effect in popular songs like "Little Green Apples," "I Never Promised You a Rose Garden," and "September Song." Caesura can have a powerfully dramatic effect, as in Tennyson's "Break, Break, Break," or Whitman's "O, Captain! My Captain!" and can thereby enhance the meaning. Run-on lines can support the imagery, as in Emily Dickinson's "I like to see it lap the miles," where the sinuosity of the railroad train winds from stanza to stanza. Similarly, the manipulation of point of view in fiction can be significant for the highly relevant question of how the writer involves the reader in his story. In no case, however, should a teacher present these technical devices as important in themselves. Nonetheless, sometimes teachers tend to do this because the technical devices are teachable and testable. They are some of the very few things that are firm within the shifting meanings and ambiguities of good literature.

More immediately important to the students' understanding are allusion and irony. Both of these devices, however, depend greatly upon the students' degree of sophistication and, in that sense, are hardly teachable as general concepts. That is, understanding what allusion is will hardly help a student in reading "The Wasteland." This is one reason that T. S. Eliot, James Joyce, Milton, Dante, and Marianne Moore are very difficult for students, and why they consequently seem irrelevant to their lives.

So much, then, for the defense of my having narrowed the field, but possibly I should defend my writing at all about elementary terminology.

Many teachers are familiar with one or another of the professional writer's magazines, such as *Writer's Digest* and *The Writer. Writer's Digest* has a "Q. and A." column each month called "Help. W.D. Answers your Questions." There is no pattern to the kinds of questions that are asked, some coming from fairly established free-lancers and rather more coming from aspiring beginning writers. A while back there was the following letter from M.H. of Pekin, Illinois:

> Q. Would you please define the term "Light Verse" for me.
>
> Also what is prose?

Now that's what I mean by the nitty-gritty of teaching literature. When I read this, I covered my face in embarrassment for M.H. of Pekin, Illinois. But the answer surprised me and humbled me.

> A. Light verse usually refers to verse that has playful, strong rhythms and rhymes, and deals with its subject in a humorous way. For examples, see the verse of Ogden Nash, Richard Armour, Phyllis McGinley.
>
> Prose is anything that is not poetry.

Writer's Digest did what few magazines and fewer professors of English will do: *Writer's Digest* answered the question. Imagine what would have been done at the *Saturday Review,* the *New Yorker,* the *New York Review of Books,* and *Playboy.* Imagine what a professor of English would have done if a sophomore had asked, "What is prose?" I knew a university senior majoring in English who asked her world-renowned professor, "What *is* your definition of an image?" I also know of another university professor whose answer to such questions—delivered amongst snorts and smirks—was some variation on the theme "you should have learned that in high school."

It may or may not be true that the student should have learned that in high school, or in elementary school for that matter, but if he didn't it's the teacher's job to help him out, rather than to bully him into not asking elementary questions ever again. That's what teaching in the classroom is all about: if there's a hole in the student's understanding, the teacher should plug it up. That philosophy of education—plugging up holes in the student's understanding—isn't so superficial as it appears, because there are many ways of plugging up the holes. One is to answer the question. Another is to guide the student to asking the question, then to guide him to means of answering the question. Sometimes a dictionary will do the job; in other cases the question will require a lifetime of inquisitiveness, as for example when the question is: "What makes a poem good?" or "Why is this novel better than that novel?" or "What is the line between art and artifice?"

Of course, no teacher can plug up the gaps in his students' understanding unless he has done so for himself. In other words, the teacher has to teach from a firm grounding in the nitty-gritty—the elementary terminology—if he is to convey to his students what literature is all about. Which leads me back to the basic terms that I want to discuss. They are literary tool-words that have currency today, but no English teacher ever got down to the nitty-gritty and defined them for me; yet these terms are as elementary as can be—and they are essential to the teaching of the humanities, since they can all be extended to other forms of artistic expression. These terms are *image, symbol, myth, fable, parable* and *allegory*. They are all, I think, compounds that share a common element. That element is *metaphor*, the most basic term of them all.

Metaphor, of course, is comparison. It is an unusual form of comparison, because metaphor does not convey more information about *two* things. When a man compares two cars, say a current model Ford and a Chevrolet, he is, to some degree, trying to learn more about both cars. But when Robert Burns writes that his "luve is like a red, red rose," the reader is not to learn anything about roses. And when Emily Dickinson writes that the sun rose "a ribbon at a time," the reader learns nothing about ribbons, and when Robert Frost says "she is as a silken tent," the reader's knowledge of tents is not enhanced. Some may be ready to point out that two of my examples are *similes*, not metaphors, and that they're incomplete similes at that. Burns did not say "my luve is like a red, red rose," but "my luve is like a red, red rose that's newly sprung in June."

As to the first objection, I'd say it's a quibble. Simile is a linguistic variation of metaphor, and the only value of the term simile is that it's so easy to teach—look for *like* or *as*—and that it provides students with a simple tool for ready identification of some metaphorical language. As to the second objection, I agree heartily. One should avoid truncating metaphors. It matters very much that the rose is a June rose, just as it matters that Wordsworth's cloud which he wanders lonely as—as which he wanders lonely—lonely as which he wanders—is one that floats on high o'er vale and hill. Fair weather cumulus is not cirrostratus.

But to return to the characteristics of metaphor: Although metaphor does not presume extensive familiarity with two things, it does require considerable familiarity with one thing—ordinarily something tangible and perceivable through the senses. *We* know roses, ribbons, tents, and clouds. What is important for understanding metaphor is that we know roses, ribbons, tents, and clouds not only literally, but emblematically as well. We've had experiences with them, and we have associative memories of them—and good writers rarely go wrong expecting certain associations. True, some people have rose fever. True, some perverse literalists might say my love has petals and attracts bees. But generally the poet guesses correctly that his readers' association will have an overall similarity. It will, that is, if the reader has had a similar experience. Emily Dickinson's line "the steeples swam in amethyst," for example, conveys little if one doesn't know what amethyst is. If knowledge of amethyst is a hole in a student's knowledge, then the teacher must plug it up. The line won't have the same meaning for that student as it does for those of us who have associations with amethyst and not just a definition and who know that the steeples didn't swim in a semiprecious form of impure crystalline quartz usually of purplish color—but it won't have any meaning for the student without the definition.

In other words, the nitty-gritty of teaching literature includes, at the beginning, making sure that the student understands what the work says at the surface level. Daffodils, clouds, amethyst, steeples, hyacinth hair, and so on, in poetry; and in prose, who are the characters, where does the story take place, and what actions occur. Sixth-grader, Ph.D., newspaper critic, and bathroom reader alike have to understand what literature says before they can understand what it may mean.

What I've been talking about so far relates only to the familiar part of the metaphor, or the vehicle of the metaphor. A vehicle carries something, as an automotive vehicle carries passengers or as the vehicle of a paint, such as linseed oil, carries the pigment. The vehicle of a metaphor carries the burden of the meaning, or, to use a musical term, it carries the tenor. The tenor of the metaphor, therefore, is the idea that we're trying to understand. It is the part of the metaphor with which we are unfamiliar. We don't know Robert Burns's love, that is, his loved one. And since we are not Robert Burns, or the persona he has assumed, we certainly cannot know immediately what his feelings were. But we do know the freshness of a June rose and we do know how receptive we are to the familiar but intricate beauty of a

red rose. We do know the soft texture of the petals of the
rose. We do know the aroma of a rose. Pleasure of sight,
touch, and smell are united in the rose in a harmonious one.
And when Burns continues that his love is "like a melody
that's sweetly played in tune," the harmony of sensations is
complete, all derived from familiar things. None of the
associations are very specific. "A melody sweetly played in
tune" is sort of a fill-in-the-blank metaphor, which might be
contrasted with a metaphor in Marianne Moore's "The Mind
Is an Enchanting Thing" that evokes the precision, intricacy,
and delicacy of the intellect: "like Gieseking playing Scarlatti." Her metaphor is not so familiar, not so vague, and quite
intellectual, but then so is her subject. The point is that both
examples are metaphors, that is, devices for enhancing and
illuminating that which is abstract, intangible, or simply
unfamiliar by means of comparing it with that which is
within one's experience.

Next, to the word *image*. I avoided this word for a long
time because it simply seemed to me to be jargon. I still think
sometimes it is jargon, communicating no more than the
preciousness of the critic. But *image* serves as well as, perhaps
better than, any other term to designate what metaphor calls
forth, and so I shall use it. The image is what is in the reader's
imagination. If the metaphor didn't work, if the reader
couldn't understand the vehicle, if he cannot imagine that
which is described or alluded to, then there is no image. The
writer may have conceived an image, and he may have
attempted to convey his conception in words, but if the
image is not transmuted into the reader's imagination, there
is no image. It's like the absence of sound where there is no
ear to transmute vibrations into tones. I think Burns's "red,
red rose" evokes an image for all of us; and I think Emily
Dickinson's steeples swimming in amethyst evokes an image
for most of us; and I think Gieseking playing Scarlatti
produces an image in relatively few of us. Of course, images

don't have to be visual, although they usually are. I think one
of the sharpest images I know of is Ted Hughes's metaphor
for the sudden recognition of an idea that has been roaming
through the dark forests of the mind. This recognition is like
"the sharp, hot, stink of fox." But unless one has experienced this sensation, the image will not exist. Image is what a
metaphor evokes in the imagination. Both terms, metaphor
and image, are too frequently confused with symbol.

I think most college literature teachers have shared my
distress at hearing students interpreting everything in a poem
or short story as a symbol. Poems, the more sophisticated
students have learned, never mean what they say; they're all
symbolic. Symbols are indeed metaphorical and they do
convey meaning as images. Symbols, however, are a rather
specific kind of metaphor. Symbols are unchanging in a given
work of literature or in a given tradition. The "bare ruined
choirs" of Shakespeare's sonnet are an image that is evoked
in metaphorical language, but the choirs do not appear again.
Shakespeare shifts from image to image, and so the choirs are
not symbols. Notice how he shifts from trees to sky light to
fire:

> That time of year thou mayst in me behold
>
> When yellow leaves, or none, or few, do hang
>
> Upon those boughs which shake against the cold,
>
> Bare ruin'd choirs, where late the sweet birds sang.
>
> In me thou see'st the twilight of such day
>
> As after sunset fadeth in the west,
>
> Which by and by black night doth take away,
>
> Death's second self, that seals up all in rest.
>
> In me thou see'st the glowing of such fire,
>
> That on the ashes of his youth doth lie,
>
> As the death-bed whereon it must expire,

Consum'd with that which it was nourish'd by.

This thou perceiv'st, which makes thy love more strong,

To love that well which thou must leave ere long.

The easiest way to distinguish symbols from other images
is to bear in mind conventional symbols. The stars-and-stripes
is a constant metaphor of America, just as the crucifix is a
constant metaphor of Christianity. The flag and the cross are
symbols. There are variations on the symbols, of course. The
conventional symbol for America, the flag, has built-in a
conventional means of showing change by the addition of
stars to the blue field as states were added. The Union Jack
of Great Britain unites conventional symbols. The variations
on conventional symbols in Renaissance religious art—St.
Veronica's veil, St. Jerome's lion, St. Sebastian's arrows, the
Virgin Mary's blue cloak, the Holy Spirit's dove—all enhance
understanding and pleasure.

Literary symbols have the same consistency as conventional symbols, but ordinarily they exist in only one work:
the scarlet letter in Hawthorne's novel, the Circumlocution
Office in Dicken's *Little Dorrit*, the whale in *Moby-Dick*, the
river in *Huckleberry Finn*, the oak tree in Sherwood Anderson's *Brother Death*, the glass menagerie in Tennessee
Williams's play, the castle in Kafka's novel, the bear in
Faulkner's stories, and so on.

One variation on the use of symbol in literary works is
that frequently symbols do not have a function of meaning.
That is, they don't necessarily stand for something, as a flag
stands for a nation's authority. In this respect the symbol
might be better called a recurrent image, but symbol seems to
be an accepted word here. The function of these recurrent
images is the same as the function of a recurrent color in a
painting; it's an aesthetic device for producing unity, balance,
and harmony—or to use a word that often borders on
jargon—for producing texture. Many modern short stories,

for example, lack the linear unity that comes from a plot line; that is, like slice-of-life drama, they lack a beginning, middle, and end, and so they make up for the apparent disjointedness by texture, or to use a different cloth metaphor, they make an all-over pattern of recurrent images. This use of texture, by the way, is a frequent device in drama and film. Symbols, in short, don't have to be profound, and teachers shouldn't be bulldozed by critics over symbols.

Thus far I've only talked about three terms: metaphor, image, and symbol. But I think that if teachers have a firm grip on these terms, and if they can transfer that grip to their students, the other terms will be easy to comprehend. Metaphor, image, and symbol have in common the characteristic of being static. They are usually points in a work of literary art. Sometimes, however, the entire work is a single image—usually called a sustained metaphor. Japanese haiku are like this, as is Robert Frost's "A Silken Tent," in which the tenor of the metaphor is a single word, the pronoun *she*, and the remainder of the entire sonnet is the predicate of the single sentence and one image. But haiku or Frost, the metaphor, image, and symbol are static.

However, if we now apply the concept of the metaphor—the concept of comparing the abstract and intangible with the familiar—if we apply this concept to a plot, we will produce a fable, parable, allegory, or myth. There is much confusion about these terms, and there is much reticence among teachers about using them, because there is much pompous claptrap among those whose profession is obfuscation. I think I can help in cutting through the verbiage.

These terms—*fable, parable, allegory*, and *myth*—all mean the same thing. They are all metaphorical stories. There is no qualitative difference between them. The *Faerie Queene*, an allegory, is worth no more than "The Fox and the Grapes," a fable, and the fable does not outweigh the parable of the prodigal son. Allegory, fable, and parable are not by nature

of their forms either better or worse than such myths as
Cupid and Psyche, or the *Ring of the Niebelung*, or Faulkner's *The Bear*.

Myth, however, is different from the other three forms of
metaphorical stories. Allegory, fable, and parable are didactic, which is to say they all have the purpose of teaching one
or more moral lesson. *Fable* is usually applied to folk tales,
children's stories, and particularly to didactic tales in which
beasts are metaphors for men. *Parable* is almost exclusively
applied to the simple fables of the New Testament. *Allegory*
probably expresses a quantitative difference more than anything, but it is particularly applied to conscious literary
productions such as *The Pilgrim's Progress*. The three terms
are virtually interchangeable, and the adjective *allegorical*
seems only to have the limitation of being applied to
conscious individual art rather than to folk art.

Myth, on the other hand, is not necessarily didactic. Art
for art's sake bred myth for myth's sake. Primitive myths, for
example, are not necessarily moral in intent. They may be
explanations of natural phenomena. The classical myths of
Daphne and Apollo or Diana and Acteon, for example, are
probably not moral in intent. And many modern stories have
a metaphorical plot—a mythical structure—even when the
purpose is not absolutely didactic. The purpose is nonetheless
mythical, for many authors want to embody elemental
human relationships in a simpler metaphorical form. Man's
inhumanity to man, sibling rivalry, the generation gap, the
quest for knowledge, universal wanderlust, the lonely crowd
syndrome are a few of the elemental drives and passions and
ambiguities of human existence that can sometimes be best
expressed in mythical form, with or without moralizing, with
or without homilies, with or without interpretation. Also, as
I shall point out in the following chapter on American
Studies, myth can be given a wider cultural meaning.

English teachers and humanities teachers whose home

base is literature may wish to pursue other technical terms, but I think that the literary terms I've defined are the most vitally elemental to the humanities teacher, because they are keys to discovering relevance in literature. Yet, the popularizing teacher might reasonably ask: What has metaphor and imagery to do with Vietnam, pot, and youth-wants-to-know? What is its relevance to the World Today?

Probably nothing, if relevance means relating literature to the events of the day. Unequivocally nothing if the events of the day means newspapers—tonight's paper, not last night's, which became irrelevant when Walter Cronkite started talking. But there are more current events than newspapers ever dreamed of. The river that Siddhartha sees in Hesse's myth is a current, and it is a current event, more relevant than yesterday's court martial, last night's automobile accidents, or the death of tomorrow's football star. Emerson wrote that the rose outside his door bore no relation to any other rose. "The sun shines today," he said. "The sun shines today also."

Literature is relevant, but nothing is relevant if it can't be comprehended, if it can't be grasped or understood. If there's a hole in the students' understanding, the teacher should plug it up. If the abstract and ambiguous problems of the day are treading vaguely around his uneasy students, the teacher can—and should—show them how that which is vague and intangible can become tangible and easier to grip if transmuted to images. Huckleberry Finn's moral struggle is more real and more relevant to us than Walter Cronkite's editorial, if the reader has imagination. Ahab didn't pursue an abstract idea, he pursued a most substantial metaphor. Siddhartha didn't find truth in abstract nouns; he found it in a river. Jesus didn't say love *mankind*; he said love your *neighbor*. And if the nitty-gritty of literary terms can make that real, then, teachers, by all means get down to the nitty and the gritty.

VII
A Chauvinist's Mirror for Man: The American Studies Approach

For reasons that have been lost in the antiquity of my memory, I never had the typical third-year high school English course in American literature. My undergraduate college education did not fill the gap, for it left me without any exposure to colonial literature and only an eight-week summer course in nineteenth-century American poetry. It was not until I was a thirty-year-old graduate student that I took courses in American literature and philosophy. I found out who I was in more ways than one, for after more than a decade of reading world literature, and particularly English literature, the reading of American novels filled me with an intense feeling of homecoming. Cooper, Hawthorne, Melville, Mark Twain—even Henry James—fitted me like well-worn blue jeans and sweatshirt. And reading for the first time Jefferson, Adams, Franklin, Emerson, and Thoreau left me with an overwhelming feeling of *déjà vu*. Like Huckleberry Finn looking at American civilization, I knew I'd been here before. I was an American, and set out to know why.

My experience is enough to assure me that American

Studies is indeed part of the humanities. American Studies is interdisciplinary, yes, but more than that, it has been for me man-centered, a relevant application to a man's life, and I think that my kind of experience is not at all uncommon. I do not feel that every American student should have a degree or even a single course in American Studies, but I do think, for many reasons, that American Studies is one of the best places to begin humanities for all students. Let me, like Dr. Franklin, begin with practical reasons.

American Studies is the most widespread interdisciplinary program that exists in higher education. Consequently, one can earn a bachelor's degree, a master's degree, or a doctor's degree in American Studies at many institutions throughout the nation and, indeed, the world. The programs differ widely, in some places only existing as equally balanced course programs in history and literature; in others, as outgrowths of sociology; in yet others, as scatterings of courses in traditional departments. Some of the major centers of American Studies exist at the universities of Minnesota, Pennsylvania, Wisconsin, New Mexico, Colorado; at Michigan State, at Stetson, at Harvard, Yale, Amherst, and Williams. At Cooperstown and Wilmington the programs are closely related to archaeology, folklore, and museum crafts; at Bowling Green to popular culture. There are programs in American Studies in Japan, Austria, Germany, France, Great Britain, and Canada. Furthermore, there are several excellent scholarly periodicals devoted to American Studies, such as *American Quarterly, Mid-Continent Journal of American Studies,* and the Canadian *Journal of American Studies.* Closely related are the *Journal of Popular Culture,* the *Journal of American Folklore,* and many regional history magazines. At a somewhat more popular level, there is the cushy *American Heritage.* In short, there is no shortage of either training or information in American Studies.

Of more immediate importance to humanities teaching, American Studies is practical because it has built-in relevance for us. There are no time gaps to leap, no language barriers to break down, no exotic theologies or political theories to stand in the way of understanding. The resource materials surround us in novels, anthologies of short stories, political documents, visual documents, local museums, historical sites and parks. Every family, every student, every immigrant is a living document in American Studies. When a student of any age writes a personal narrative, another chapter has become part of the American heritage. Less obvious, but more profound, is the fact that American experience is not isolated from the larger humanities. Born of the Renaissance, the Reformation, and the Enlightenment, America's culture provides a common experience from which one can move into the European past. Familiarity with Jefferson, for example, can prepare one for Locke and Rousseau; Transcendentalism can be an introduction to Platonism. Furthermore, the melting-pot mixed backgrounds of Americans can fire interest in the music and arts of Africa, South America, and Eastern Europe. American public architecture surrounds every American with a displaced classical world. And despite some thin spots here and there, American poetry, painting, music, novels, and philosophy are worthy of study and appreciation in their own right, as well as for indigenous training in techniques for understanding the arts of other cultures.

But this welter of advantages and achievements makes American Studies a potentially hazardous approach to the humanities. The most obvious danger is chauvinism. Allied to this is provincialism. Just as the danger in celebrating the achievements of Afro-Americans is that some students, black and white, will begin to think that Black necessarily means Best, so celebrating the achievements of all American artists will breed in some students the wrong-headed idea that American means Best. The study of America can provide touchstones for looking at the rest of the world, but it must not presume to provide an absolute standard for judging the rest of the world. James Fenimore Cooper is not better than Jane Austen; Emerson is not more profound than Kant; Ernest Hemingway does not threaten Thomas Mann; Charles Ives will not supplant Debussy; O'Neill does not make Ibsen irrelevant. Teachers know this, I know it, and yet in my own teaching of American Studies I get occasional feedback that warns me that the message that got through to my students was not the one I sent out; and I suspect other teachers have had the same experience. I am not distressed about the student who comes to me after a class to say, "You tell us that Emily Dickinson and Frank Lloyd Wright are great artists, but how do I *know* it?" I am, though, concerned about the students who don't challenge me, and who aren't suspicious, for I fear that some of them may think my message is a variation on the chauvinistic theme of "America—Love It or Leave It." That thought brings me to another hazard of American Studies, professional disillusionment.

College teachers and students are more likely to fall into this hazard than into chauvinism, because their training in criticism tends to exclude emotional responses. Also, it is simpler to explain what is bad about someone's achievement than what is good about it. Look over the comments your professors wrote on your college themes, and you'll see what I mean. American political and social thought is filled with loftier statements of ideals than other nations have been adolescent enough to make. Americans cherish exceedingly noble ideals of equality, brotherhood, democracy, individualism, will of the people, free speech, rights-to-life-liberty-and-the-pursuit-of-happiness-give-me-your-tired-your-poor-God-Mother-American-apple-pie-flag. Humanists know that America has not succeeded in living up to these ideals. But many Americans are not humanists, and they are surprised, and I think, a little bit hurt to learn that America has not achieved the perfection it seems to claim as its own. Sometimes they become angry, and sometimes they decide that it is the ideals that are ridiculous, and, rather paradoxically, they conclude that the Americans have been traitorous. I don't usually agree, for like all humanists, I often see life as a tragicomedy, of poor forked creatures reaching for the stars. Martin Luther King had a dream that I think will never be fully realized, but the dream is not ridiculous. Neither do I regard my vain, feeble, misplaced attempts to implement the dream as negations of the ideals. My abortive attempts are only human.

While the dangers of chauvinism and of debunkism in the teaching of American Studies are always present, they are usually easily discernible. A more insidious danger in American Studies is not seeing the forest for the trees, or vice versa. Teachers and their students are products of American culture, and live in the middle of the culture that produced them; this makes it very hard for teachers—and for all Americans—to see themselves and their immediate environment in perspective. The tendency is to err either toward a near-sighted or a far-sighted focus. In the near focus, localism predominates, and the American experience is viewed in the terms of the immediately familiar. In the far-sighted focus, the familiar is viewed with contempt, and the local scene seems provincial, conservative, unimaginative, anti-intellectual, certainly not worth studying.

To see the forest and the trees at once in focus is not an easily acquired skill. Thoreau at Walden managed to see the restricted surroundings of Walden as a part of all eternity, and he managed to see himself as a part of mankind. Emerson distilled the idea down to the title of a poem, "Each and All." A friend of mine who lives in San Francisco put it well. He was driving me across the Golden Gate Bridge; above us was a jet plane, beneath us some ocean ships. "It always makes me feel like the cover of a social studies book," he said. That is the essence of each and all. It is being in the forest and seeing the forest, at once. It is being the individual thinking "I" and seeing himself as the merest part of the big picture, at once. It is being Neil Armstrong as a man and mankind, at once. It is being the dancer and the dance, the spectator and the spectacle, the chessman and the game, all at once. This is not a perpetual experience, for no man believes anything twenty-four hours a day. No man is a Member of the Human Race his every waking minute. No man is always man thinking, for sometimes he is man hungry for a hamburger with everything on it, sometimes he is man looking up the telephone number of the Ford garage, sometimes, alas, he is man defecating. But there are times when one does see himself as a member of the human race, when one knows he is the forest and trees. This vision may be precipitated by a public event, such as the moon landing, or the assassination of Dr. King; it may be precipitated by reading *Oedipus Rex* or the Bible; it may be the sudden recognition that our little lives are rounded with a sleep.

This mystical experience, though, is not truly the teacher's province. However, it is the teacher's province to prepare the student in the intellectual correlative of the forest and the trees paradox. In American Studies, the teacher must make the student recognize his heritage and his experience as being American. The teacher must help him to objectify his experience, to stand off from it and to regard it with detachment and with interest. This purpose sounds less mystical than those of the previous paragraph, but it is no less difficult to put into practice. It is an easy thing to speak of a mirror for man, but it is not easy to construct the mirror or to resolve an image within it. In a general sense the mirror-construct of American Studies is *myth*, which is to say it is the recognition that the apparent contradictions in the American value systems are resolved in metaphorical patterns of belief. Thus, the American Studies approach selects symbols, icons, and myths, and thereupon attempts to discover the meanings that have been attached to these metaphors by Americans. The practitioner of American Studies is of course interested in the empirical, logical, factual truth, so far as it can ever be ascertained; but he is equally interested in what Americans have believed to be the truth.

Although there were in the 1930's a number of important works that incorporated this American Studies approach (for example, Constance Rourke's *American Humor*; Dixon Wechter's *The Hero in America*), the "bible" of American Studies is Henry Nash Smith's *Virgin Land* (1949), in which Professor Smith explored what the American West was, and what Americans believed it to be. In this interdisciplinary book, he made use of such varied source materials as political speeches, serious novels, dime novels, paintings, poetry, legal documents, personal narratives, and folklore. A similar classic of American Studies was written by one of Henry Nash Smith's students, John William Ward, who, in *Andrew Jackson: Symbol for an Age,* documented some startling discrepancies between the "real" Andrew Jackson and the transformed version of reality that made him a demigod. In these works, as well as in the many other first-rate works in American Studies, the aim is not to debunk heroes and cherished beliefs, for myths are not lies; they are simply other ways of expressing truths. Rather the aim of American Studies is to discover deep-seated social-psychological truths as they are expressed metaphorically, both in "high" artistic expression and in popular and folk expression. That is what lies at the base of all American Studies, and that is what is applicable to any other nationalist or ethnic studies.

But before any teacher, particularly a teacher of secondary school students, leaps into this type of American Studies, let me warn that it is the deep end of the pool. First, a teacher can't start playing off myth against reality until his students have a firm grasp of both history and literature. Second, analysis of myth and symbol is highly sophisticated work, as I've tried to show in the previous chapter, and it requires experience and proficiency in literary analysis and iconology. Third, American myths are very close to students, and what begins as objective and dispassionate analysis of social-psychological phenomena may descend to wanton destruction of important personal values. That is, stereotyped simplistic faith can easily be converted into stereotyped simplistic solipsism. Solipsism in itself isn't bad; indeed, I rather think that it is an important stage in intellectual development, but it is irresponsible for a teacher to lead a student down a corridor to an empty room with no exit. It is a method analogous to that of the college freshman English teacher who set out to teach her students that their favorite work of literature, Joyce Kilmer's "Trees," is a bad poem. What a waste of time! Why not teach why Shakespeare's twenty-third sonnet is a good poem? Then her students would like *two* poems.

Despite these warnings, the American Studies approach to the humanities remains the most practical starting point in humanities teaching. In addition to its immediacy, its built-in relevance, its wealth of available materials, and its lack of exotic cultural barriers to understanding, American Studies is undoubtedly the most flexible in level of difficulty. It is possible to construct a highly erudite course in American Studies that places very limited literary demands on students. Moreover—and here is one of the many puzzles about the American experience—the nonliterary course need be no less sophisticated, subtle, or humanistic than the erudite course. The basic reason for this is that, regardless of America's many instances of racial, ethnic, and religious bigotry, regardless of the inequality and class identifications that are an uninterrupted current in American history, the essential American experience is common to all. Walt Whitman's "Song of Myself," in which he is himself each and all, recognizes this truth in its unified catalogues of Americans of all "classes." Ralph Ellison came to recognize that the American Negro's experience is an American one, not African, not Asian, not alien. The commonality of the American experience, then, causes its cultural expression to be similar in the evocations of folklore, of the popular ethos, and of serious artistic works. The serious artist, of course, is more efficient than the folk or popular artist, for he knows consciously what he is doing. In other words, to approximate with popular materials what Mark Twain does in *Huckleberry Finn* would require a mountain of frontier ballads, slave songs, pioneer diaries, temperance pamphlets, sentimental samplers, architectural and home-furnishing photographs, proslavery sermons, dime novels, and folk tales. Commonality of experience, however, does not mean simplicity, a point that is especially important to remember when one is dealing with myth, for myth puts a childish mask of simplicity on the face of complexities that transcend logic.

It is possible to assemble a short reading list that, properly read and analyzed, can stand for American Studies. Three books will do the job: Benjamin Franklin's *Autobiography*, Thoreau's *Walden*, and Mark Twain's *Huckleberry Finn*. Lest some complain about roads not taken, let me explain what I mean by properly read and analyzed. The New Criticism approach of the previous chapter on reading literature applies here, for teachers must begin with what is there, in each book, before they can centrifuge off to interdisciplines. This is not the place for detailed examination of the three works, but it is worthwhile to look at some of their general characteristics, all of which imply something of the American experience. First, they are all first-person books written by highly independent anti-aristocratic individuals. They are all in some sense simple books (although Huck Finn's dialect can be troublesome), but in each case the simplicity is deceptive, and deliberately masks hard-earned art under the guise of easy and humorous narrative. They are all based on a Christian Protestant heritage—indeed, they are White-Anglo-Saxon-Protestant—but they are all unchurched and irreverent, and they are all youthful. All are autobiographies, but all are fictional. That is, they may tell nothing but the truth, but they don't tell the whole truth.

Severally, too, the three books cover the sweep of

American culture. The *Autobiography* is urban, *Huck Finn* is small town, *Walden* is wild. Franklin is materialistic, scientific, and group-oriented. Thoreau is idealistic in both the popular and the Platonic senses, and he is fiercely independent of society. Huckleberry Finn is unintellectual and a social outcast. Franklin is self-educated. Thoreau has two Harvard degrees, and Huckleberry Finn is a Sunday School drop-out. Put them all together, and they spell American Studies: first-person, individualistic, anti-aristocratic, simple, humorous, WASP, unchurched, irreverent, youthful, urban, small-town, wilderness, materialistic, scientific, group-oriented, idealistic, antisocial, unintellectual, outcast, self-educated, college-educated, and literate elementary school drop-out. Humanities, as I have said, is dissonant; myth, as I have also noted, is illogical.

Each of these three books provides a base from which the teacher may make forays into other areas of American culture, all of which can give the student perspectives on his own life and culture. From Franklin, for example, one could move back to the Massachusetts puritan colonial society from which he came, or one could take Franklin's ethic of business success as a theme and move forward through the variations in success literature of Alger, Howells, Dreiser, Steinbeck, Nathanael West, LeRoi Jones. Or, one could take the allied theme of the self-made man and examine means of self-education, requisites for rising socially, and material symbols of success, in such various forms as etiquette books, advertisements for correspondence schools, deodorants, and hair-straighteners, in the Sears and Roebuck "wish books," true romance magazines, and high society movies. From Thoreau, one could pursue themes of the Transcendental creative tradition (which can lead to such varied artists as Emerson, Frost, Frank Lloyd Wright, and Andrew Wyeth); or one could pursue the theme of the wilderness (with an easy step to conservation and pollution); or one could shift from the independence of *Walden* to the commitment of *Civil Disobe-*

dience, with myriad contemporary correspondences and variations. From *Huckleberry Finn*, one could strike out into the fields of minority groups and the WASP establishment, particularly if one also included in the course Twain's *Roughing It*, which is probably the best compendium of American prejudices that exists—Indians, Chinese, Irish, Catholics, Negroes, Mormons, dudes, ministers all get their "due."

This three-book approach is not, of course, the only method of organizing an American Studies course. In fact, although I have used a dozen or more methods in planning American Studies courses that I have taught, I have never used this method. What the teacher does all depends. What he does may depend mainly on the limited reading ability of his students, in which case he might do well to explore some theme for which there are many nonliterary sources available, such as Images of the American Hero, easy to teach using movies, television programs, comic books, adventure stories, popular songs, tall tales, and folk songs. Other themes that might lend themselves to nonliterary examination are Images of the City (particularly rich in photography, black poetry, popular music—with many opportunities for nonliterary creative expression with cameras and tape recorders) and Frontier Life (with many sources in museums, folk songs, and films).

Even in the more formal literary approach, the built-in relevance is never far away, for the problems considered and encountered by Franklin, Thoreau, and Huck Finn are both perennial American problems and more general, larger humanistic problems: What is success and how can I achieve it? What is my relationship to nature and the landscape? How much do I owe to my fellow man? Underlying these questions are three more basic questions of the humanities: What is a good life? What am I to do with my life? Who am I? In short, American Studies need not be provincial, and self-investigation need not be culturally narrowing.

The question of who am I appears to be purely egocentric and divisive, but in reality it also looks outward and seeks harmony. In every man's search for an answer to that question is a hope for the brotherhood of man. Tolerance and understanding can probably be achieved as well by studying other faces, other places, other dreams, but such exotic worlds are all mere hollow pedantry if one does not know himself. American Studies held up a mirror to me, a mirror in which I saw an American, and I saw that being an American has made all the difference. Not only am I an American, I am an American from eastern Wisconsin—Manitowoc, in fact—and that has made a difference, too. Moreover, I was a South-Sider, from Riverview, and we lived on the gully side of the street, where one eye always opened to a little wilderness of hips and haws and a clear view of the setting sun, and that has made all the difference.

One can't go home again, but never, never can one escape home, and that is why you are you, and I am I; and in our separateness is our equality and our brotherhood; for when I come to respect myself, I cannot but respect you too.

VIII
From the Beatles to Brahms:
Popular Culture and Mass Aesthetics

Although many of the questions of the humanities have not yet been answered, many others have been answered, and, to a certain extent, the answers are what constitute the high school or college "survey" courses in history, literature, Western civilization, art history, and philosophy. These courses are the end result of selection, analysis, classification, disputation, and rejection of events, persons, and documents. Eventually an area of study achieves what appears to be a satisfactory set of answers, and this is manifested in standard textbooks that predominate in the field through many editions. The asking of humanistic questions does not cease after the standard surveys have been set, but the questions do tend to become excessively precise and restrictive. Thus, for example, the questions relating to the poet John Milton and his works possibly started with "Is Milton a great writer?" and "Is a Christian literary epic possible?" and went to "What is Milton's conception of the Fall?" and "Which is Milton's most representative poem?" to "What are the classical analogues of 'Elegia Sexta'?" and "What is the

97

significance of the variant spellings of *be* and *me* in *Paradise Lost?*" As answers to questions like these develop and become incorporated into standard courses, some humanists begin to look for other areas in which the unanswered questions are broader in scope and interest. A result of their researches is that, from time to time, the settled survey courses and the standard texts are drastically revised, even replaced, as new answers are found. In the various humanities these processes are constant because humanists work with history and the arts, and there is new history and new art every year, all of which will be analyzed, judged, classified, and argued about. In addition, the humanities are in a continuous roil because the humanities are concerned with questions of taste, fashions, and other value judgments. Consequently, humanities courses are filled with instances of declines, falls, resurrections, and discoveries of cultural eras and personages.

Philosophy, for example, currently shows some indications of a shift in emphasis from strict positivism toward metaphysical systems, particularly of the Orient. Art historians are pulling nineteenth-century romantic paintings out of museum basements. History and literature are finding room for black and American Indian achievements. Musicologists are searching for the place to put electronic music. And humanities courses are turning from standard histories of Western civilization to interdisciplinary studies that include the non-Western world. One broader area for investigation of new questions in the humanities is popular culture, which in one respect or another is engaging interest in all of the humanities.

The term *popular culture* is most readily understood as a development of mass production for a mass audience, and as such is primarily a phenomenon of the last two centuries. There are earlier instances, of course, but the acceleration of technology has made popular culture the predominant cultural environment today. Another way of defining popular culture is to distinguish it from folk culture, which is local and traditional, and from cultivated or "high" culture, which is individual and self-conscious. Some illustrations might help to explain. The individuality of "high" art can be exemplified in a painting by Rembrandt—or even by an anonymous artist like the Master of the Barberini Panels—where we are aware of the artist's personality. This is not the case in a work of folk art—let us say in a Navajo sand painting—or in a work of popular art, such as a Campbell's tomato soup can label. The self-consciousness of "high" art appears in the theoretical and self-analytical statements of artists, for instance in Henry James's prefaces to his novels. Folk and popular artists are not *un*conscious, of course, but their explanations rarely go beyond statements that "it is always done that way," from folk artists, and that "that's what the public wants," from popular artists. Some additional three-part examples may help to clarify the definitions. In cultivated music, there is Beethoven's Eroica Symphony, in folk songs, "Barbara Allen," and in popular culture, the Mantovani-Muzak version of "Love is Blue." In architecture one could contrast Frank Lloyd Wright's Falling Waters house, a Transvaal N'Debele thatched hut, and a Levittown "rambler"; and in sculpture, Rodin's *Hand of God*, an Alaskan totem pole, and a plastic Jesus. In each of these groups, the first example is individual and self-conscious, the second is local and traditional, and the third, mass-produced.

But the distinctions between popular, folk, and "high" culture are neat only in definition, rarely in practice. That is one reason that popular culture studies are full of question—mass-produced popular items sometimes slide into folk traditions (singing commercials replace nursery rhymes; "Kleenex" replaces "handkerchief"); and some "high" culture items turn into mass-produced popular items (reproductions of great paintings sold in dime stores; Edgar Allen Poe's "Annabel Lee" converted to a popular song). In addition, the definitions become confusingly intertwined when a highly individual cultivated work like Richard Wagner's *Tristan and Isolde* is recorded, and the recording is played on the radio for a mass audience. That is an academic tangle, however. But there are problems that relate more directly to the theme of this book. The first of these is: Does popular culture have a place in the teaching of humanities?

It does, if for no other reason than that the American student's cultural environment is almost entirely constituted of arts that are purveyed to him as a member of the mass audience. There is very little of pure folk culture remaining, with its traditional transmission of techniques and products from generation to generation. For most students, "high" culture is remote and institutionalized, not really a part of their immediate environment. Consequently, the students' cultural experience and their aesthetic standards are within the realm of popular arts.

If it is accepted that popular culture is one of the legitimate concerns of the humanities, we are ready for the next question, which is the general subject of the rest of this chapter: How can popular culture be used in the humanities course?

Popular culture sources in teaching are ordinarily used incidentally and allusively; and both kinds of uses are quite defensible, for the popular arts are generally stereotyped and discursive, and they usually contain only a limited number of characteristics and techniques that require to be taught or discussed under a teacher's guidance. More important, because we all live in a world of popular culture, an allusion is all that is needed. The students, being steeped in popular arts experiences, will accept the allusion and they will have a clear image because the allusion is so familiar.

It is this familiarity, the immediate evocation of a clear image, that makes popular art forms appropriate for use as introductory sources. If, for example, a humanities teacher is pursuing the theme of the hero, he need hardly do more than drop the names of recent or current television series heroes:

Mannix, Max Smart, Bugs Bunny, the IMF, and Matt Dillon. The clarity of the familiar television image can serve as a catalyst for achieving understanding of Odysseus, or Don Quixote, or Leatherstocking, just as a picture of a hyacinth from a flower catalogue may catalyze understanding of Poe's "To Helen." Similarly, the local post office building may provide a familiar architectural lead-in to the classical experience or to the early national period in United States history. The rock opera *Jesus Christ—Superstar* or the film of *Carmen Jones* can provide a lead-in to the study of grand opera. These last three examples, federal architecture, *Jesus Christ—Superstar*, and *Carmen Jones*, are, of course, high culture popular art forms—that is, they have a conscious aesthetic purpose, and they are none of them mass-produced art forms in the sense that comic books, television serials, automobiles, or cigarette packages are mass-produced—but even the most mundane popular art forms can serve as catalysts. Cigarette packages, for instance, might be a useful lead-in to a study of such a matter as conventional symbolism and, thence, to religious art. What does the white of the package symbolize? Why aqua colors on Salems? Why a camel? Why a penguin? Why names—none of which have logical or lexical significance—such as Marlboro, Chesterfield, Benson and Hedges?

Familiar images, then, can be effective in preparing students for understanding more remote or exotic or specialized art forms. Familiarity, though, can also breed contempt, so popular sources should be used with a light hand, and any teacher who designs a course to deal exclusively with popular culture must be aware that the students' familiarity may produce a barrier to understanding. The barrier arises because the objects and terms of popular culture may seem to students trite and negligible, not legitimate subjects for serious discussion, as I discovered in a college course in popular culture that I taught a short time ago. How serious the problem can be was brought home to me by the comments of two of my students, who, at the end of the quarter, told me that they had for a considerable time thought that I was crazy to be talking about Johnny Cash, William S. Hart, Petula Clark, and Sandwich glass cup plates. Obviously, then, the teacher's first task is to mark out the legitimate problems of popular arts and the legitimate areas for exploration.

I'm going to talk in more detail about my course, not because I advocate specialized courses in popular culture, but because I think my experience may provide some guides for judicious use of the popular arts in other courses, both in traditional disciplines and in the humanities. Before I explain the content and methods of my course, I'd best set forth its context, because some of my methods were determined by the curricular context within which I operated.

My course is the envy of many of my colleagues and, I suspect, the laughing stock of others. It is open only to juniors and seniors, and because I fulfill my fiscal obligations to the school in a giant lecture course for sophomores, I can justify restricting the enrollment to a maximum of twenty. This matters, because I think popular culture should be studied by small groups and by individuals, rather than under mass instruction conditions: The topics of popular culture are inherently controversial, and students must have maximum opportunities for discussion and disputes. My course does not lead to a major degree, and so I am not obliged to guard the arcana of a profession. This also matters, because it makes it possible for the students and me to follow our noses. The students come from all disciplines, and this varied clientele matters too, because the students bring in lively disputes argued from the prejudices of their major fields, and I think that they are more effective in broadening one another's viewpoints than I am. Last year, for example, the class included one very solemn philosopher, two home economists, two English majors, an impassioned *artiste*, two Canadian hockey players, who I presume majored in something else, a speech major, and an utterly baffled young chemist.

The course was highly structured in my mind; but I never let on. It's easy not to let on in a course in popular culture, because the content is infinitely wide and varied, and therefore it is very easy to follow the students' leads in finding objects for discussion and analysis. The subjects and purposes, though, were mine, and underlying them all was the simple purpose of all my teaching, which is to show that the world is an interesting place. Not good, necessarily; not bad; not progressive, necessarily; not necessarily crumbling either. Just . . . interesting. Now, upon this simple premise, I conceive that in a humanities course I am teaching human beings, all of whom will have an influence on other people, and some of whom will become teachers—and that matters to me very much. One cannot be a human being without self-respect; one cannot be a teacher without respecting others. One cannot respect himself or others unless one also respects his own culture, popular or unpopular. So, if my students can someday go into the ghettos, or to the Indian reservations, or to the middle-class suburbs and make others there look at their own cultures as worthy of interest, as worthy of criticism, and as worthy of serious investigation, it may be that self-respect will ensue, and then the ends of humanistic education will have been served.

I have a dream, too, although I don't push it, for I might break my heart. In my home, I am a cultural snob, and it is my dream that through a genial investigation of popular arts my students will have their critical and aesthetic sensitivity heightened and sharpened, and that they will slide effortlessly into higher arts and higher culture. I dream that they will be larger beings, taking pleasure in the beauty and variety of the world, which is an interesting place. I hope, too, that they will suffer, as I do, the ecstatic pangs of aesthetic dyspepsia.

Now, some brass tacks. Here is how I organized my course:

First, I exposed my students to the legitimate areas and questions of popular culture.

Second, I employed group projects as a means of building experience and confidence in dealing with popular arts.

Third, I set the students free.

As to the first, I violated my usual principles and began with secondary sources. My reason for doing this was that, by means of showing the students good scholarly essays on popular arts, I hoped to demonstrate that it is possible to be serious about that which is familiar, cheap, and apparently trivial. Without such exposure, I fear that a course in popular culture might descend to mere antiquarianism, camp cuteness, and contemptible gossip. I used three textbooks: James D. Hart's *The Popular Book*, Norman F. Cantor's and Michael S. Werthman's *History of Popular Culture*, and Irving and Harriet Deers' *Popular Arts Critical Reader*; and I also placed on reserve copies of the *Journal of Popular Culture*. My use of these texts was eclectic and pretty much up to the students, but let me explain how Professor Hart's book was used.

First, I asked the students to read any chapter that they thought might interest them. Second, I asked them to read any one of the books mentioned in their chapter. Third, I asked for a short oral discussion of the book in the light of what Professor Hart said and in the light of such questions as: "What does the popularity of the book tell you about the society that made it popular?" and "What standards of taste does the book suggest to you?"

In addition to secondary sources, I presented for discussion and definition a number of common and conflicting terms, most of which are adjectives that might modify either *culture* or *art*. The terms are: *classical, elite, folk, kitsch, mass, popular, vernacular,* and *vulgar*. My purpose was not to present or develop hard definitions, although it was of course necessary to root out total misconceptions. What I had in mind was cutting out loose talk, as well as exploring the aesthetic judgments inherent in assigning any of these labels to an object.

The first exposure to primary source material was the book that each student had selected from Professor Hart's work. There were other primary sources that I presented, along with my comments and analyses. For popular artifacts, I used about one hundred slides that I had made from some of the *Life* magazine filmstrips of colonial, frontier, and Victorian arts. I arranged these chronologically, pointing out such characteristics as decorative motifs derived from religious and political viewpoints (Bible verses on Puritan pottery; playing cards illustrated with American national heroes); the effects of mass manufacturing techniques on design (lacy glass to mask mold marks); the survival of obsolescent forms in design (the carriage form of early automobiles). Related to the slide presentation was a lecture and film on Currier and Ives in which the techniques of mass-produced art and the domination of popular taste in determining art content were discussed. The film was *A Trip With Currier and Ives*, already mentioned in Chapter V; here, however, I used it not as a primary source in itself, that is, as film *qua* film, but as an extremely effective presentation of Currier and Ives pictures. The sound track is composed of folk songs (including some "pop folk," such as Stephen Foster's "Nelly Was a Lady") sung by Tom Glazer, and thus the film does double duty in presenting two popular arts genres.

I extracted triple duty—or maybe even quintuple duty— from other films. (I should mention in passing that I never use audiovisual "aid" films: I believe that films must always be primary sources, not substitute teachers.) Among the other films that I used were some clips of Buffalo Bill's Wild West show, *The Great Train Robbery*, and a group of William S. Hart westerns. With these, I was able to consider such things as the development of camera and acting techniques in the art of the film; the concept of the western hero; the impact of the movies on earlier forms of mass entertainment. The filming of Buffalo Bill's show juxtaposes two traditions, one dying and one just beginning to thrive, for it was the advent of movies that brought about the extinction of Wild West circuses. There may be real significance in the closing scene of *The Great Train Robbery*, in which the gunman shoots the audience. The William S. Hart clips provided introductions to popular American myths, and from there it was but a step to some of the essays in the Deers' anthology, such as John Williams's definition of the western as myth and Robert Warshow's essay "Gangster as Tragic Hero." In discussing music I also made use of films, particularly John Cohen's brilliant documentary on Kentucky mountain music, wherein folk and popular traditions are presented side by side: Child ballads, Elvis Presley, lined-out hymns, and Coca-Cola live together in uneasy harmony.

That closes part one of the curriculum, in which the purpose was to expose the students to the legitimate fields of investigation and to some essential questions and definitions. The second part of the course was a group project that I used as a preliminary step toward individual projects. This group project I consider to be the most unusual and the most successful part of my course, and the one which I think might be most profitably copied and adapted to different age groups and curricular contexts. My reason for using the project was to pattern for scholarly investigation of objects in the popular arts. A pattern is needed, because, as all teachers know, students sent off alone into research often lack confidence in their abilities to make aesthetic judgments; or, much worse, they become overconfident, and uncritically gush forth stereotyped generalizations founded only on old prejudices. They rarely know how to extract large questions from restricted subjects, and not many are given to sharp self-criticism. This sounds like professional bitching, but it must not be construed as contempt for students. As a teacher, I know that it is my task to identify the gaps in my students' knowledge and fund of skills, and thereupon to plug up those gaps. I do not despair at my students' inadequacies; indeed, I am much more distressed at the nightmarish prospect of finding a class before me without such weaknesses and inadequacies—they are the *raison d'être* of a teacher.

To explain how the group project worked, I'll simply set forth the instructions that I gave to my students. They may sound rather restrictive, but if one bears in mind that the purpose is to provide a pattern for investigating particular objects, and that the pattern must obviously be adjusted for different genres, I think that the requirements are not unreasonable.

GROUP PROJECT: POPULAR ART AND ARTIFACTS

1. The class will be divided into groups to examine, to discuss, and to make a class presentation on certain assigned primary sources. The first class-hour is for brainstorming and assigning research problems; the second is for preparing a report.

2. Some guiding questions for small-group consideration:

   Is the article art? Was it conceived as an object of art or of utility?

   Is it popular art?

   Is it folk art?

   Is it vernacular art?

   Is it kitsch?

Is it manufactured, that is, machine-produced?

If so, has the manufacturing technique determined any of the aesthetic values?

What restrictions has the manufacturing process placed on the article?

Whether the article is handmade or machine-made, what raw materials and techniques are used?

To what class did it appeal?

To what class might it still appeal?

Are the reasons for the appeal different? If so, why?

Do you like it? Why? Are the reasons within you individually? Or within you as a member of a class? Or within you as a member of a generation? Are the values by which you judge it subconscious or deliberately learned (in this course or some other)?

What more information do you need?

Where can you find the information?

3. Each group must assign its members significant areas of research. Here are some suggestions for assignments. Do not assign more than two persons to a given task.

Find and study an essay or chapter in one of the applicable textbooks.

Examine the various bibliographies (both dittoed and printed in your textbooks) for other sources.

Check libraries or museums or second-hand stores for similar artifacts. Compare and contrast.

Question local authorities—artists, professors, antique dealers, oldtimers. (Note: Specialized information possessed by authorities is a marketable commodity. You must respect professionals and their reticence about giving free information. This is particularly true of price appraisals.)

For library research—in card catalogues, *Readers Guide, Art Index, Humanities,* and *Social Science Index,* etc.—here are some *general* headings you might consider:

> Technology, History of
> Popular Culture
> Aesthetics
> Mass production
> Content analysis
> (And, of course, the general name of the object at hand)

4. Each group must hold at least *two* more meetings. The time, place, and length of the meetings should be determined by the group. The usual classroom and the usual class time is of course available, but a group may find it worthwhile to meet in a library study room or reference room, or at a museum, or possibly at a secondhand store. (Note: Behavior appropriate to such meeting places must be maintained. Students must accept responsibility for any damage they cause. Do not use fountain pens near rare materials.)

5. The last meeting of each group should be devoted to the method of presentation. This may be a panel discussion

(formal or informal), the reading of a joint report by one member, a lecture-demonstration by one or more, etc. If there is dissenting opinion in a group, provide for minority statements.

6. Time schedule:

    First meeting ———————————————————
    Regular class meetings canceled ——————————
    Report and discussion meetings ———————————

7. Your instructor will *only* provide reference and bibliographical information. All value judgments and aesthetic controversies should be hashed out in the group.

Naturally, there is no end to the possible objects that could be considered, but I used a flatiron, a carnival glass bowl (a beastly thing that my students found to be worth over fifty dollars), and a restrike of a Henry Clay commemorative Sandwich glass cup plate. All of these things happened to be around our house, but I did not select them haphazardly. I wanted old things, because it is easier to be objective about them than about contemporary things: students have already made up their minds about electric can openers, *Playboy* covers, Blenko glass, and T-Birds. I also wanted concrete objects that could be handled, passed around, and kept static while being discussed. Thus, music, films, and books were omitted from consideration because they all have a temporal dimension and are consequently unwieldy. Finally, I wanted the objects to exhibit some of the characteristics that we had been discussing.

Here I also would call attention to one of the most legitimate questions in humanities: "Do you *like* it?" I cannot remember ever having been asked this in a college class. Yet for what reason do we study the arts if we are not to project ourselves into the objects or, conversely, to see what is mirrored of ourselves in the objects? On the other hand, I remember the frustration of being confronted in elementary and secondary school by the undying "book report" question: "Which part did you like best and why?" The questions that I ask in the second part of the assignment sheet are all designed to help the student answer the humanist's poser: "*Why* do I like what I like?"

Before taking leave of the group project, I think I might discuss the adaptability of this means to different curricular contexts. Its adaptability to elementary school use is obvious, since my project is nothing more than a sophisticated form of "show and tell." I am told that there is a movement afoot toward specialized teaching in the primary grades, and this is most regrettable, for who then will take on "show and tell"? Which specialist will say, "Find something from the culture in which you live, and we will respect you and your culture if you will tell us about it."

At the high school level, I would suggest eliminating the secondary source textbooks. The teacher, though, should become familiar with the discipline of this new interdiscipline of popular culture, and himself serve as the secondary source. I also would suggest repeating the group project in a pattern of progressive complexity, as from static artifact to objects with a time dimension, such as television programs or popular music.

In high school and college, both the content and the purpose can be readjusted to specialized fields. Thus, in a history course, the emphasis can be placed on recreating the popular ethos of the period. I have done this with a very successful project in which local historical museums were used for studying artifacts that show a response to the American frontier environment (barn-door hinges made from horseshoes; "snowshoes" for walking through swamps). In a literature course the use of popular fiction is obvious. In a sociology course, the emphasis can be shifted from questions of aesthetics to such problems as discovering the caste function, or fetishistic function, or symbolic function of the popular object.

This now completes the discussion of the second stage of my course. As for the third stage, explanation is hardly needed. I simply set the students free to pursue their own projects. Whatever the student wanted to do was approved by me. I dismissed the class for two weeks and reserved the class period for unassigned conferences, which were frequent.

I hope that my students learned something valuable from this course; I think they did. I know I learned several things from this study of popular arts. I learned that intelligent criticism of popular arts cannot be made by those who are devoid of experience in aesthetics. I learned that just because one lives in a popular environment one is not thereby qualified to make aesthetic judgments on that environment. Popular art forms are more stereotyped than "high" art forms, yes; but even such apparently simple forms cannot be intelligently evaluated without the techniques of literary criticism, art criticism, and cinematic criticism. There are a variety of reasons for my saying this, the first being that there is not yet any generally accepted body of critical techniques for the study of popular arts. In addition, I have read popular arts criticism written by some journalists and social scientists whose lack of familiarity with cultivated parallels and historical influences, combined with glossing over of details of language, visual symbolism, and camera techniques, can lead to oversimplification, misplaced enthusiasm, and, occasionally, downright error. Another reason for my insistence on critical practice in the popular arts is that oftentimes popular arts replicate the "high" arts in modified forms; for instance, carnival glass, which has its antecedents in Tiffany ware; religious calendar art, which has Renaissance antecedents; and Classic Comics, which are obviously based on classics.

These examples suggest some further problems in the use of the popular arts in the humanities course, problems of aesthetic judgment that will increasingly plague teachers as they incorporate more and more popular sources in the classroom. One danger is overemphasis on popular material, which can lead to the exclusion of the great universal works of mankind. It might be argued that my course in popular culture did this, but then mine was primarily a course in methodology. The *general* humanities course, however, has a larger purpose, that of incorporating our new technological culture into the mainstream of human achievement.

That being so, the modern humanities teacher faces the dilemma of maintaining a balance between popular culture and certified "high" culture. The old hens who insist on the subjunctive and who breathe starrily and noisily along with Beethoven and Browning represent one unbalance. They live only for classics sanctified by time, and give their students an unreal, ethereal view of culture. At the other extreme is the svelte swinger who continuously dignifies the latest entertainment fad of his students with higher criticism; he may be doing no more than reinforcing their adolescent prejudice and limited cultural experiences. It is true that "I know what I like" equals "I like what I know." It is also true that there can be great impact in helping students to learn that maybe they don't really *know* what they know. But the teacher who uses this method must recognize that he may not be markedly widening his students' cultural horizons by dwelling on popular forms.

In short, the teacher must strike some sort of happy medium between the old hen and the svelte swinger if he is to avoid presenting his students with a highly distorted view of culture and the arts.

This much might well be granted by most teachers—and I think it is—with at least relative equanimity. But the questions that immediately arise about how and when to use the popular arts in the classroom are emotionally charged questions involving cultural biases and personal preferences. Let me clear the ground a little. Since the aesthetic techniques required to assess "high" art are probably more concentrated and require more training than those used to evaluate the popular arts, it would, I assume, ruffle few feathers to apply the "high" techniques to popular arts, to go from "high" culture to popular culture. Close analysis of Brahms would contribute to understanding and enjoying the Beatles; skillful reading of Dostoevsky would help one discern philosophical and psychological insights in the *Peanuts* strip. But what about vice versa? That is, can knowledge of the elements of popular art be as profitably transferred to "high" art as the "high" techniques can be to popular arts? Obviously the popular arts can serve as good introductions, can engage the interest of students in artistic expression; but will more extended study of popular art provide useful techniques for more sophisticated forms? I have no final answer to this, but the question can never be answered if it is not tried, and a trial is not possible unless teachers set aside their biases against popular art. I think that those who are unwilling to begin with popular art—and here is where the individual emotional response and snobbery really enter the picture— balk principally because of their bias against the use of certain popular art forms. One might, for instance, feel strongly pro-Beatles, quite willing to make it the *four* B's of classical music, and yet remain unwilling to issue a passport to Parnassus for *Peanuts*.

If my assumption that most people's strong feelings are attached only to a limited number of art forms is correct, then the final point I want to make here is best approached in the form of several concrete alternatives, some of which may touch individual cultural sore spots, but some of which can be considered without one's cultural prejudices getting in the way of the answer. My question now is: Which direction would be more helpful in promoting understanding and appreciation of the following?

   1.   From Dashiell Hammett to William Faulkner, or from William Faulkner to Dashiell Hammett?

2. From Norman Rockwell to Edward Hopper, or from Edward Hopper to Norman Rockwell?

3. From Billy Graham to Reinhold Niebuhr, or from Reinhold Niebuhr to Billy Graham?

4. From the "Andy Griffith Show" to *Our Town*, or from *Our Town* to the "Andy Griffith Show"?

5. From Jerome Kern to Gian-Carlo Menotti, or from Gian-Carlo Menotti to Jerome Kern?

Weighted questions, aren't they? I've weighted them both for quality and popularity: the popular items represent very high quality work, and the "high" items are all popular, particularly in terms of their durability over time. They're all American; all fairly recent but not so recent as to confuse matters with faddishness. In every case, one item of each pair represents popular culture in three respects: with respect to mass production (paperbacks, record singles, magazine covers, and so forth); with respect to popular traditional background (Kern developing from the musical-comedy light opera-operetta tradition, Billy Graham coming out of the itinerent evangelist tradition); and with respect to adaptation of subject, scope, and technique to meet the requirements of the largest audience (for example, simplicity of language, use of sentimentality and patriotism, restricted size or length). The other item of each pair represents "high" culture with respect to marked individuality (as opposed to adherence to a severe pattern); with respect to complex forms and deliberate subtlety; and with respect to being rooted in older traditions than the popular items (or at least demonstrably older traditions).

Now, let me return to the question, which was not "Which is better?" The question was, "Which direction of learning would be more effective, from high to pop, or pop to high?" The answer of most teachers may well depend upon their knowledge and the relative sophistication of their students. My answer, however, depends on the theme of this book: humanities for *all* students. I would move from popular to (let's face it) unpopular, and then, occasionally, back again. A teacher who gives serious attention to the students' familiar surroundings, and who helps the student to know more about what he likes, can lead in from the popular art to look for similar characteristics in the unpopular art form. In popular music, for example, the average listener does not recognize recurrence of themes or patterns: he is aware of them, but he cannot identify them—and this applies in most cases even to the simplest form of verse and refrain. Also, few listeners will consciously separate group performances into their component parts of instruments and voices. Doing only these two things with popular works—listening for themes and learning to recognize component parts—will make it an easy jump to fairly simple symphonic works. These things should be done, though, as an intellectual exercise in perception, not as an emotional or aesthetically valued experience. Just as in poetry one must read the words that are there, on the page, before arriving at images, interpretations, and possibly enjoyment, so in more complex forms of music one must begin by simply hearing what is there. The humanist teacher can't *teach* pleasure. He can, though, try to see what difficulties might stand between his students and their taking pleasure in art, and then do what he can to remove the difficulties.

IX
Humanities Other-Directed and Inner-Directed: What to do Until the Doctorate Comes

The only way that I can outdo William Shakespeare is that, while he possessed only small Latin and less Greek, I possess no Latin and no Greek. I don't have a swelled head about it, though, and just as you have promised yourself to keep up your French—someday—or to read the *Divine Comedy*—someday—I regularly promise myself to remedy my linguistic ailment—someday. But my ignorance of the classical languages serves one useful purpose: it symbolizes to me the fact that I can't know everything. This is a humbling fact that any humanist must recognize, for without such recognition, his intellectual sin is very great, and he deserves as punishment to have his liver picked out daily. On the other hand, habitual admission of ignorance can turn into a handy excuse for doing nothing about curing ignorance. One must distinguish between being a professional in the humanities and a professional in the humilities. The world has never become better because of men who are proud of their humility.

If one aims to become a professional humanist and

interdisciplinarian—and this aim means being in some sense a teacher—one condemns oneself to walking a cobweb beset with a myriad of crossings, forkings, and roads not taken; and every road not taken is to some degree regretted. The dilemma of the professional humanist is that of being a nonspecialized specialist, of being a disciplined interdisciplinarian. The curse of the professional humanist is that he is reviled as dilettante, eclectic, and jack-of-all-trades by professionals in the component humanities; and often he deserves the revilings, for when the humanist scholar leaves his proper plane, the cobweb, for the straight and narrow tightropes of pure literary criticism, or pure musicology, or pure political history, he is sure to teeter, he will probably totter, and it is quite likely that he will fall. The interdisciplinarian must bear in mind that he has, of his own free will, chosen to specialize in not being a specialist. As a scholar, he will more often consult other specialists than will more traditional professionals such as theologians, logicians, or art historians. Nonetheless, the professional interdisciplinarian need not be apologetic for his ignorances, for he possesses very specialized talents and postures of mind that delineate his own province among all the professionals in the various humanities.

The cobweb province of the professional humanist is one of *themes, variations,* and *correspondences.* This is what privileges him to violate national borders, to break through traditional departmental barriers, and to roar up and down the centuries. This does not, however, privilege him to redo the traditional disciplines. When a political scientist says that in paragraph X political theorist B shows his indebtedness to political theorist A, or when an art historian says that painting Y is the product of painter Z's later period because his brush stroke shows characteristic D—the professional humanist must believe them. And when a musicologist, an art critic, a literary historian, and a sociologist all use the technical term *impressionistic*—the word should be understood as each specialist means it in his peculiar context. The humanist, on the other hand, might consider, for example, such a term as *impressionism* as a theme, and thereupon consider its variations and correspondences among the various disciplines, always with the ultimate purpose of relevant application to men's lives. How one can attempt some preparation for such tasks is my subject in this chapter, and I shall make suggestions for institutional preparation in humanities as well as for humanities self-taught. Before I do, though, I should explain my apparent equivocation about two terms I have been using, *teacher* and *scholar*.

In some senses, the sanctimonious cliché that every teacher should be a scholar is true. It is true in the sense that a teacher cannot ever stop acquiring knowledge, a fact that needs strong reinforcement in the face of one of the greatest abuses of the teaching profession, the syndrome in which, like Will Rogers saying that "all I know is what I read in the papers," teachers act as if they believe that all they *need* to know is what they learned in college. Some years ago, I sat in on a high school English Department meeting where the topic was how many book reports should be required from each student in each grading period. The consensus was two, but it was a grudging consensus. I knew many of those teachers, and I also knew their reading habits. They read *Time* cover to cover, and felt informed; they read the *New York Review's* "Letters to the Editor," and felt liberal; they read the *New Yorker* fillers, and felt sophisticated; they read *Reader's Digest*, and didn't admit it. Mainly, they read student themes. In this same high school, the Art Department required a faculty show each year, and, at the time, I thought that if I ever chaired an English Department, I'd require book reports of the English teachers. I've never been a department chairman, though, and now I think that even if I were I wouldn't have the courage to ask my staff for book reports. For one thing, I've heard some teachers' book reports. For another thing, such a practice smacks too much of "publish or perish," about which I have many ambivalent feelings, among which is the feeling that the policy takes the joy out of research and writing. "Required" reading for professional teachers would, I'm afraid, run quite counter to the joyful energy of humanistic investigation. As "publish or perish" oftentimes produces trivial notes, pedantic patter, and divided, subdivided, and sub-subdivided dissertations among the imperiled professors; so required readings would produce page-counting, blurb-reading, and reviews of reviews among secondary school teachers. No, the humanist teacher must be a scholar because that is his way of life. *Docta ignorantia*, a sense of curiosity, a desire to satisfy that curiosity, and a drive to tell others all about it are the requisites for the humanist scholar.

Note particularly the last requisite, the drive to tell others all about it. That is what conjoins teacher and scholar. There are some scholars who do not crave an audience. For them, scholarship is unrelated to teaching. They collate texts, publish newly discovered letters, and indulge in such projects as "Critical Reception of Picasso's *Guernica*, 1937-1942." Their projects are not contemptible, nor are they useless, except in the sense that a ten-penny nail at the bottom of a bin in a hardware store on Christmas Day is contemptible and useless. The nail and the "pure" scholarship is not humanistic, for the humanist's province demands relevant application to men's lives. That is why the humanist needs an audience, although the audience need not be a congregated class. A writing, publishing humanist scholar has an audience, but it may consist of only ten men over a century's passage of time. The humanist teacher, on the other hand, operates in the present and reaches for a larger audience. Thus the real distinction between the humanist scholar and the humanist teacher is twofold: The teacher's audience is here and now, and the teacher's audience has a lower level of common knowledge, while the scholar's audience is usually scattered in time and space and possesses a common fund of specialized knowledge. There are two points I would stress. First, the scholar is a humanist only insofar as he has the goal of relevant application to men's lives (but not necessarily every man's life); second, pure scholarship is part and parcel of humanistic scholarship. You've got to have the nail in your hand before you can clinch it home, and the humanist scholar may sometimes need years to gather and assemble materials before he can apply them. Translations, collations, bibliographies, summaries of critical receptions of *Guernica*, and published preliminary studies may be needed before relevant application to men's lives can be achieved. Two of the most mind-opening examples of humanistic scholarship are John Livingston Lowe's *Road to Xanadu*, in the literary field, and André Malraux's *The Metamorphosis of the Gods*, in the field of religious art.

For most teachers, however, humanistic scholarship does not yield the ocular proof of a magnum opus, or any published works at all. For them, the results are most apparent in the continuously changing content and methods of the courses they teach, and less outwardly apparent in the increasingly heightened, broadened, and more sharply focused delight they take in the world around them. The results are also frustratingly manifested in increased *docta ignorantia*.

Humanist, teacher, scholar. The words are all for one and one for all. So how does one become prepared to be a humanities teacher? At present, there are very few institutions of higher education that have a curriculum designed to develop humanities teachers, and only a few states are working toward designing certification standards. At present, most humanities teachers in the public schools and in the colleges were prepared to be English teachers. This trend is likely to continue for some time to come, and that is the reason that I have directed some of my suggestions toward English teachers. Without having gathered any statistics, I would hazard a guess that, in descending order of frequency, the college preparation of those teaching humanities in secondary schools has been in English, history, art, speech, foreign languages, and music, while the preparation of college teachers has been in English, history, classics, philosophy, speech, art history, comparative literature, and American Studies. The situation couldn't be better, at least in two respects: Virtually every humanities teacher today has a firm and disciplined grounding in the techniques and content of one of the traditional humanistic studies. Virtually everyone now teaching humanities has come to the humanities point of view from his own inclination, and it is more than likely that he has had to carve out a place in the curriculum himself, alone, and against the prevailing currents of education. In short, humanities teachers of the fifties and sixties have been highly motivated. High motivation begets enthusiasm, enthusiasm begets high student interest; high student interest begets a positive educational environment.

Nonetheless, now is the time for the training of humanities teachers to become institutionalized. My statement may seem to be a heretical contradiction in terms, but since we have already arrived at the point at which school systems are looking for humanities teachers to hire, we can no longer wait for these teachers to evolve by natural selection. When the fad of humanities hits a school board or a dean, or when student demand insists on immediate change, if there are no institutionalized standards for teacher preparation, there will be assignment of ill-prepared and utterly confused and often antagonistic teachers to humanities classrooms. I have attended many humanities conferences, workshops, and conventions in which the majority in attendance were just such baffled teachers. This phenomenon can be observed more dramatically in the Black Studies movement, where huge demand has been frustrated by almost no supply.

Critics of the humanities movement will, I am sure, call all this a tempest in a teapot, claiming that the demand has been small, that humanities is only an ephemeral fad, and that the demand will decrease rather than increase. They may, of course, be right, but I think that their vision is narrow. The humanities movement is but one aspect of the temper of the seventies, which will continue the trend toward disenchantment with specialization. Humanities, ecology, and medical general practice all reflect the temper of the time. In each of these areas, students, professionals, and the general public have discovered that specialization, while over-whelmingly efficient in producing short-term results, has in the long view produced anomie, confused priorities, and alienation. That which in more innocent days might have been called an unmitigated good in a technological innova-tion is seen today as equally productive of friction, feedback, noise, pollution, and heaven knows what other side effects. In medicine, we have found that treating the salient symptom not only may ignore a basic cause, but may also produce an unforeseen chain of unpleasant consequences. Detailed exam-ples need not be spelled out here, but consider these innovations, all of which, in one way or another, have proved to have wide-ranging and unforeseen (or foreseen but ignored) consequences: wide-spectrum antibiotics, DDT, oral contraceptives, television, expressways, Volkswagens, jet-liners, *Playboy*, nuclear power, transistors, credit cards, ster-eophonic recording machines, detergents, long-playing records, paperback books, xerography. These have variously produced changes in manners, morals, politics, law, educa-tion, health, recreation, religion, and social and personal psychology. In natural sciences, we have learned that we must look at the whole environment. In medicine, we have learned that we must look at the whole man. In education we are learning that we must look at the whole man and his environment—physical, psychological, sociological, and cul-tural. In all of these, the humanities teacher has an interest, but his specialized nonspeciality is the interaction of the individual and his cultural environment.

Institutionalization of training for humanities teachers is fraught with dangers. The greatest of these dangers is the possibility of rejection of the natural humanist. Allied to this is the danger of the development of an educationist establishment, a cult of unimaginative, secondary-source bureaucrats. It is a very real danger, since professional humanists are anti-institutionalists and loners, while professional educationists are a bandwagon crowd, highly skilled in the implementation of the iron law of oligarchy. Past experience has shown, too, that the professional educationist, however well-meaning, unjustifiably assumes a *camino real* to knowledge content; or so it seems as he emphasizes how to teach rather than what to teach.

But dangers aside, let me get down to brass tacks. For preparing a college course of study in humanities, I can think of only two requirements (not counting the character and intelligence of the student himself, and those of his professors): Every student needs a world chronology, and every student needs experience in creative expression. As to the first requirement, the chronological course, it doesn't seem to me to matter what kind of course it is. A chronological humanities course would be fine, but a course in cultural, political, or even military history would serve the purpose. Wars, unfortunately, occur at such frequent intervals that the whole gamut of world chronology can be covered militarily. A chronological course in world literature would probably be better, because each work of literature is highly individual and, as a consequence, more memorable than secondhand historical data. A chronology of art history might serve, but given the manner in which most art historians teach, with slide projectors running like a Gatling gun and nary a map or political reference to take the student out of the darkened chambers, the usefulness of an art history chronology (as the single *required* chronological touchstone) depends heavily on the teacher's being oriented to the humanities. Music history has the disadvantage of commencing only a thousand years back. A philosophic-religious chronological survey would be excellent, except for the fact that the chronological segments are more widely separated than those encountered in "straight" history or literature.

The purpose of the chronology should be readily inferred from the above: It is to place an orderly array of hooks and hangers in the closet of human experience. It provides a place to hang a newly learned bit of knowledge. A sense of chronology guards against (but cannot always prevent) putting Robert Browning on a motorcycle or Cleopatra in a pyramid. Such misconceptions are always possible, and all of us, even professional historians and humanists, receive occasional chronological shocks, such as finding Michelangelo, Moctezuma, and Sir Thomas More to be contemporaries; but many shocks can be forestalled by a good grounding in chronology. I do not think that it is important that dates be memorized, but it is important that any humanist have a feeling for the historical parallels and sequences of events. It is also important that a chronological course be required, for I am sure that it is possible in many colleges today to avoid any study of the world before Columbus, and I suspect that it is in some schools possible for a student to confine all his cultural studies to the United States.

The second requirement in the institutionalized training of a humanities teacher is training in creative expression. I wouldn't waive this requirement for anyone, but, on the other hand, I wouldn't require success of anyone either. It's the participation in some form of creative expression that's important. My often inharmonious fling with the cello and my adventures in art class, where I used to add rocks to my landscapes because I was always dropping paint in the wrong spots, did not make me an accomplished cellist or painter; but my experiences in both music and painting were humanizing, and I think they have prevented me from becoming a totally arrogant critic. A humanist must understand that there are technical restrictions to creative expression. I am not saying that one must find "good" in everything, nor am I saying that it is valid rebuttal to say to the critic, "Could you do any better?" What I am saying is that it is pure arrogance to teach the importance of creative expression without having tried it oneself.

But what about the student who is a musician, and maybe even a composer? He should be put in an art studio course, or a creative writing course, or a cinematics course, or a dance course, or a course in stagecraft, or acting, or photography, or radio, or television. If the student is already a published writer, he should be exposed to piano lessons, or any of the other expressive forms mentioned. In "grading" the experience insofar as preparation as a humanities teacher is concerned, effort is more important than achievement. In the process, the Humanities Department may lose some students, either because of stunning discouragement or sparkling success, but either way, the humanities will be better off.

Beyond the two basic requirements, there are many desirable kinds of courses, in literature, art history, music appreciation, philosophy, and, of course, interdisciplinary studies. I would urge a basic course in cultural anthropology, good courses in psychology, and a course in original readings in the history of sociology and political science. Another kind of course that would be of estimable value is one in the history and philosophy of science. The humanist is deeply concerned about the achievements of man, and much of the story of human achievement of the last two or three centuries is in the realm of science, which has altered the environment and thought processes of contemporary man. Most science courses today, however, ignore science as a study and concern themselves with the specialized preparation of professionals. In view of the dearth of scientist teachers, it may be that the humanist teacher will have to assume as much of this function as his ignorance will allow. This is not a desirable practice, for, as I have said, the disciplines *are* disciplined, and what is needed here is a humanistically-oriented scientist, not an amateur. The problems implied here are basically twofold. First, how does one institute a training program for humanities teachers where many desirable courses are nonexistent? Second, how is one to provide for interdisciplinary cooperation among component departments?

The ideal single solution to both problems, it seems to me, is the creation of a department of interdisciplinary studies that includes the natural and social sciences as well as the humanities. Within this department should be a pool of interdisciplinary-oriented professionals from the traditional departments, as well as a core of professionally-trained interdisciplinarians. The department should regularly offer introductory basic courses, specialized interdisciplinary courses, and culminating seminars and projects, but a major burden of its work should be farmed out among the traditional departments of the college. In other words, the interdisciplinarians will have the task of introducing students to the idea of pursuing *themes, variations, correspondences,* and *relevant application to men's lives.* They will have the task of helping students determine what traditionally disciplined training is desirable, and they will have the task of aiding students in discovering interrelationships among the specialized courses that they have taken. The pool of interdisciplinary-oriented specialists will have the task of serving as consultants, advisors, members of lecture series, panels; and they will be called on to prepare special interdisciplinary courses, such as "Philosophy of Science," or "Cybernetics and Social Change," or "Classics in the Modern World," or "Aesthetics of Urban Life," or what have you.

Flexibility must be the only absolute in a department of interdisciplinary studies. This department must, more than any other branch of a university, be willing to admit to errors and be willing to bend in the direction of student interests and social change. It must not play the numbers game: if one student in an institution of ten thousand desires a major in wilderness park planning, this department must help him, guiding him to courses in such subjects as geography, botany, sociology, recreation, geology, transportation, American Studies, aesthetics, Emerson and Thoreau, landscape painting, and city planning. In such a student's case, a semester's credit for travel, or land-clearing, or survival-training, or all of these might be recommended. In most cases, however, students don't know exactly what they want; yet, on the other hand, they quite reasonably object to their teachers' claiming to know. For these students, recommended alternative courses of study with suggested patterns of electives will provide directed flexibility. But a first-year interdisciplinary humanities course seems essential, if only to show the variety of courses and areas of study that exist. Today's high school students appear to be sophisticated, but I think that most of them still enter colleges with a restricted idea of the realms of knowledge. A century back, college education meant law, theology, or, less often, medicine. A decade ago, it meant being a doctor, a nurse, an engineer, a teacher. And even today, students need to be made aware that there are such professions as anthropology, social psychology, popular culture, ecology, urban planning, astrophysics, classics, art history, comparative literature, area studies, and, of course, humanities. As a teacher of humanities, every year I meet college students who, on the verge of graduation, discover themselves to have misspent four years because of their ignorance of the variety of possibilities. Dispelling this ignorance is not a job to be shunted off on high school guidance counselors, nor is it a job to be done with a list of vocations or even a college catalogue. It must be done by *showing* the students what drama criticism is, what art analysis is, what cybernetics is, what history is, what psychology is—but the options need not be shown in "preprofessional" courses. They can be shown in a battery of interdisciplinary courses, in which the various disciplines are used as they relate to themes and problems.

By now it must be clear that I am not either revolutionary or innovative. I have spoken of very traditional aspects of higher education. I have not set out to destroy courses, credits, departments, traditional disciplines, lectures, courses of study, guidance, or requirements. The kinds of institutions, departments, and courses of which I speak already exist and, in a few places, have existed for half a century, though they are scattered, too rare, and inadequately supported. However, the existing institutions tend to ossify and entrench; and often they become elitist, tending to set a hierarchy of values. My proposals are aimed at avoiding such rigidity and snobbery, for both are antagonistic to the humanist's goals.

The snobbery evinced, for example, by the English major who bows only to classics, and deigns to nod only to physics and philosophy and possibly comparative literature, is anti-humanistic because it rejects other fields of investigation. (Avoiding such elitism does not, of course, mean that one cannot criticize the shortcomings of those working in another field—so long as one does not condemn the validity of the discipline itself. I have in this book spoken slightingly of educationists and sociologists, who are often regarded as the two greatest offenders of clear literate expression, but in view of the fact that this book on humanities is actually a work of sociology and education, it must be clear that I do not reject or denigrate those disciplines.) The humanist must maintain respect for all areas of knowledge. He must never fall into the trap of believing that his wide-ranging skills, interests, and courses replace semester-long courses in Milton, the anatomy of the shark, social aspects of alcoholism, or Pre-Raphaelite painting. These are different in kind, in scope, and in breadth of application from humanities courses, but they are not different in absolute value.

As for rigidity, it must be combated because it prevents the openness to the world and to ideas that characterizes the true humanist. The humanist, and the institutions training humanists, must insist on flexibility. This is hard to do because it entails taking a chance on being wrong, but it is imperative that the humanist be allowed freedom in his investigations, freedom from rigidity and from elitism.

But what to do until the doctorate comes? What is humanities inner-directed? How can the teacher trained in a traditional discipline be self-taught in humanities? In three words, the answer is he can read, look, and listen. He can read novels, plays, stories, phonograph record jackets, magazines, biographies, histories, textbooks, anthologies. He can look at art shows, television, movies, museums, plays, and faraway places. He can listen to music, to lectures, to radio, to conversations, to noise. Then he can train himself to find themes, variations, and correspondences and bring what he has learned to his classroom. In the Appendix, I have listed some sources that one could use as a core from which to work outward. They will provide one way to keep self-teaching from scattering in all directions, but it is only one way. A better way is for the teacher to identify some hole in his knowledge and plug it up. One of the three ways to organize a humanities course—as problem studies, period studies, or area studies—might be applied to the teacher's own self-education. He could set a goal of Renaissance Studies, Classical Studies, American Studies, Mythology, Images of God, Romanticism, Popular Culture, Expressionism—whatever. He could read a basic book, or take a college course, and follow the leads they provide. He could travel to relevant places, if possible; or study a foreign language if it seems necessary.

Apropos of that, many of my readers may already have noticed the absence of a foreign language requirement. Although I feel that such a requirement might be justified, my experience as an advisor has been that the requirement that a student learn a foreign language is a fetish and is rarely a humanizing or mind-broadening experience. I've never met a man who became interesting, tolerant, or humane just by learning another language. I have, though, met interesting, tolerant, humane men whose acquaintance with a foreign language has made them *more* interesting, *more* tolerant, and *more* humane. The same goes for foreign travel. A dullard who goes to Europe is still a dullard. A bigot who goes to Europe is still a bigot.

Of course I am exaggerating. I'm not saying that to become a humanist one should stay home and speak English. And nowhere have I claimed that a course in art history or English literature will necessarily make one a sensitive lover of the arts and literature. However, a hard look at foreign language study will show that it is a time-consuming—though not necessarily time-wasting—preparation in a *tool* for further humanistic study (and the same is true of science laboratory experience). I am not speaking of graduate education in the humanities, but of the undergraduate preparation of humanities teachers, and for such a purpose, time might be more profitably spent in exploring the many fields of human achievement and investigation than in laborious acquisition of tools whose immediate application is limited in scope. Just as learning to dissect a shark is of little value in studying inorganic chemistry, so learning to read French fluently is of no value in reading haiku. For most purposes in teaching humanities, written materials are available translated into English, which is a singularly rich language. The ideas of the original and, to a considerable degree, the artistry of the original, can be communicated in English. However, there are exceptions to this, the most notable one being poetry, and for studying these exceptions a foreign language is indicated. A humanist would want to pick the least narrowing language, and that, I think, is Latin. It is true that by the time one has mastered sufficient Latin to manage a sensitive reading of Catullus, one is no closer to Basho, Homer, Akhenaton, Li Po, Heine, or King David. But it is also true that one *is* closer to reading Michelangelo, Chaucer, Dario, Mallarmé, and many, many others. Because it opens so many doors, Latin is undoubtedly still the most efficient and valuable foreign language that a humanist can command, and, therefore, any college that is going to require a foreign language of its humanities students should require Latin.

In fact, I think I'll get at studying Latin myself. Tomorrow, if it rains.

X
The Teacher as Egotist:
The Pied Piper of the Humanities

Any of my readers who has taught school at any level knows that there is a notable discrepancy between that which has been taught and that which has been learned. Inhumane teachers—and there are many—assume that the discrepancy is a product of the student's perversity. Inhumane teachers seem to believe that students rise each morning, stretch, and say as litany, "What can I do to be incompetent today?" Humane teachers, however, do all that they can to narrow the discrepancy, and that is why good teachers are always "revising" their courses and presentations. Humane teachers also learn to treasure the more humorous examples of dissonant understanding, not because these instances exalt the teacher, but because they humble the teacher and caution him against presuming too much knowledge and experience on his students' part. Let me illustrate from my own teaching experience. In one of the first stops of the 1970 National Humanities Series, I was, through a fluke in scheduling, placed before an assemblage of two hundred fifty eighth-graders. All of my prepared remarks were designed for adults, but I was flexible, and dropped easily and happily into my old role of junior high school teacher. The kids were wonderful, and so was I. I did a short commercial on the National Humanities Series and thereupon did an impromptu soft sell on poetry. Their attention was flattering; my ego was expanding. And in the question period that followed, the first question was from a bright-looking little squirt who wanted me to tell more about the "Humane Society" that I represented.

So I answered his question.

I also thought about what had caused the boy's misapprehension. Not, surely, willful ignorance, but simply false expectation. My lecture, like every humanistic presentation, be it a class or a work of art, existed in an environment of expectations, not in a vacuum. These expectations consist variously of definitions, prejudices, stereotypes, clichés: in short, they consist of prior experiences. The eighth-grade boy had, quite wisely, latched onto the word *humanities*, which was not in his experience. "Humane (Society)" was, though, and heaven only knows what adjustments his mind was making in the forty minutes during which he attentively gave ear to what he supposed to be a representative of the SPCA who talked about the relevance of poetry. There was, in other words, a wide discrepancy between what was taught and what was learned, because I had not anticipated his expectations, which were totally rational, but based on ignorance—not, as inhumane teachers would assume, on perverse and total ignorance, but simply on a hole in the student's understanding.

The little boy's question was what teachers call a "dumb question" (I saw his teachers cringing in embarrassment, possibly even in unwonted guilt); but I know, from years of teaching experience, two things about dumb questions: First, they are republican questions, that is, they are highly representative, and thus the one boy probably spoke for a majority, which, in that case, meant at least 126 people.

Second, dumb questions are an essential part of good teaching, for they are the teacher's only real device for learning about his students' expectations, misapprehensions, and prior experiences. They are the teacher's most efficient form of feedback. They inform the teacher of intellectual derailments. They tell the teacher when students have transferred to dead-end spur lines of understanding.

Don't get me wrong, though. I am not exalting stupidity, and I am not justifying the many useless questions that result from inattention and laziness and the cliché questions that are deliberate time-wasters designed to sidetrack a teacher and to get the class off the academic hook. These are show-off questions, and I'm sure that sophisticated adolescents could put together a handy list of them, headed, at present, with: "What is the relevance of [fill in the blank]?" My point is only that teachers must take note of and respect and answer questions that point to basic inadequacies in prior experience. Some years ago, for example, while I was dilating upon some profound mythical meanings in William Bradford's *History of Plimmouth Plantation*, a college student asked me what *divers* (diverse) meant, and since that time I have always done a little teaching of reading—of seventeenth-century prose—before embarking on "college" teaching. Recently, I illustrated some points about American black aesthetics with a recording of an early rural blues song, and I saw, too late for remedy, in the faces of my audience that they did not know how to listen to blues, nor, for that matter, how to listen to a scratchy old 78. Another example: Again and again, I have found that while most average Americans don't know how to look at an abstract painting, those others who are products of art courses in design and abstract painting are unschooled in looking at representational art; they are often incapable of piercing through surface reality to apprehend the abstractions that lie beneath.

In all these cases, some gap in the students' understanding constituted a barrier that prevented them from appreciating the art work in question. Art, in other words, is not universal, at least if we are to understand universality as inherent in all men. Before art can be truly appreciated, there must first of all be a common base of expectations. To a certain extent, these expectations develop naturally out of a given culture, for a given culture. But for most people in any culture, at any time, the body of expectations—the usable conventions of expression—is limited, possibly in direct proportion to language vocabulary. I doubt, for instance, that Billy the Kid could get much meaning from Aaron Copland's music. I doubt that Leonidas the Spartan could get much meaning from a Nigerian fetish figure. I doubt that Garibaldi could get much meaning from Bix Beiderbecke. I doubt that Gyuka, a nineteenth-century carver of netsuke, would get much meaning from Andy Warhol's Campbell soup can. I also doubt that I would have found much meaning in the Sermon on the Mount, if I'd been there at Jesus' feet. I don't know Hebrew, and William Bonney never heard a symphony orchestra, and Gyuka never saw a soup can, and Leonidas was probably still trying to figure out Phidias. In each of these cases, clearly, the work of art does not speak for itself, does not convey much, if any, meaning to the perceiver. And in each of these cases interpretative training and analysis would be needed before understanding could be reached.

The point is not that the artist does not infuse his work with a clear meaning. Artists, I am convinced, speak as plainly, clearly, and simply as they can. But all artists must select some medium of expression before they can speak, and that expression will be in a conventional medium that cannot communicate meaning without common understanding, any more than a foreign tongue can communicate without understanding of the conventions of the medium, which is to say, the language. (It is true that we can understand foreigners somewhat through sign language, gestures, and facial expressions, but these, too, are based on conventions of expression, which, as paralinguistic studies show, are not so universal as brotherhood buffs would have us believe.) The point is that without learning the conventions of expressive media, one can confront a work of art only with ignorance and can expect to extract little, if any, meaning from it.

Lest one object that my previous examples of the need for a common basis of understanding are too exotic and far-fetched, let me demonstrate the un-universal nature of some media that are closer to home. Movies, one might suppose, are a universal form of communication that can be comprehended by all men in all times. So I would have imagined, had I not learned, half a dozen years back, that radio listening, which I had assumed to be immediate to all, required a complex battery of expectations and conventions. Today, to young people, radio-drama listening would have to be taught. My son is a being of the television age, and when he heard, for the first time, a classic radio drama, he was dismayed and baffled by time and place transitions that were expressed by music, and by the "telephone-voice" technique of expressing inner thoughts and flashbacks. In a similar fashion, all of us today are so accustomed to visual wipes, cuts, pans, close-ups, spinning scenes, superimposed images, and the like that we assume that these are universal language. But students of cinematic history inform us that audiences, as well as actors, were quite thrown by early close-up shots of human beings. On stage, one had always seen the whole actor.

In other words, works of art do not speak for themselves. That is why humanities teachers—including specialists—are needed. The place for dumb questions, for learning about the conventions of expression, is the classroom, not the concert hall or art gallery or movie theater. It is in the classroom that students—all of us—build up the common expectations that are necessary before true appreciation of art and true humanistic experience are possible. Works of art, like humanistic presentations, cannot project meaning into a vacuum; they have to be apprehended. Thus, works of art are mirrors for mankind. In a work of art we apprehend not only what is *out there*, but what we bring to the work of art. That is the truth of the hackneyed saw that "you only get out of it what you put into it." That is also the reason for the simplistic idea that "a work of art is what it means to you." But neither of these means much if there is no, or mistaken, input. That, again, is why the humanist teacher is needed. Needless to say, humanist teachers do not aim to be taste-makers, aesthetic bullies, or opinion-mongers. Humanist teachers are only trying to provide their students with tools for individual interpretation. Humanist teachers are only trying to build an informed body of expectations among culture consumers. Humanist teachers are only preparing students for independent humanistic experiences in which what they put into the experience is their *own* relevant experience, not ignorance, local prejudice, or narrowing misconceptions.

When aiming toward informed apprehension of art works, humanities teachers often begin with popular art works, because all students, by virtue of living in our culture, have some body of expectations, however elementary and emotional, to apply to popular art works, some way of perceiving themselves in these mirrors for man. As I said earlier, though, teachers must be careful that presentations of popular art do not bog down in mindless nowness; such presentations must lead *in* and, further, lead *on* to wider perception. In other words, humanities teachers cannot, in their efforts to reach all students, abandon intellect, analysis, or the past, for to do so is to narrow the brotherhood of man to here and now, to popular prejudices, to hip humanities, and to empty-headed emotionalism. This is an exceedingly important point, for, as I said, humanities teachers are pied pipers, and as they work with popular culture, the lively arts, and hip humanities, they must not confuse popular applause and a parade of marching followers with humanistic ends. Charisma is a method, not a goal. It must be borne in mind, therefore, that pop culture, hip humanities, and lively arts are means to an end. A thoughtful end. I have observed some of the humanities courses in frenetic aesthetics, and, even where the material chosen is of high quality and is tastefully correlated into a multimedia year-long show, I wonder if it has maturity as an end.

The trouble with the world is that we haven't enough grown-ups. I'm not talking about birthdays or age or physical maturity or intelligence quotients. I'm talking about grown-up human beings; people who value their lives, because they know their lives are short; people who value all lives, because they value their own lives. People who retain the freshness and joy of life of youth; but not the puerility of the childish "me first"; "gimme, gimme"; "I want"—the childish emotional response.

Humanities teachers must make certain that their classes and methods produce grown-up human beings, not well-bred shaggy dogs (like the one I own), whose gamut of emotions is limited to sleep, boredom, excitement, and vigilance. They must recognize that the excitement of being enveloped in a psychedelic world of unmeaning sensations is a gut reaction, of which anything with a gut, from the phylum Annelida to us higher anthropoids, is capable. They must recognize that the vigilance of carrying a placard or viewing with alarm is a group gut. Even the Annelids will group and demonstrate together if one puts the heat on.

Grown-ups think. Grown-ups think, and that's why they are incapable of boredom. Grown-ups do not confuse lack of sensuous excitement with lack of stimulus. Grown-ups think, and analyze, and compare, and contrast, and store up, and do not make a decision only on the basis of the report of the first precinct. The lively arts have value only insofar as they contribute to the art of living, only insofar as they become part of the art of living.

In my travels with the National Humanities Series, the only thing that horrified me about human beings was the incestuous feeding of prejudices. Racial prejudices I saw, and I was saddened by the sight, but I was not surprised. However, I was shocked when I saw senior citizens, men and women whose lives were near an end, feeding one another's prejudices, nourishing one another with hate for youth, and for posterity; and when I saw professionally young people—some balding and graying—feeding young people the cult of the NOW, the feces of the moment, spoon fed with only the fleeting relish of newness; and when I saw teachers presenting the past in the prejudices of the present. All this is the opposite of humanities, for in the humanities we must assume other eyes of other peoples, other places, other times, to look at the present.

To use a contemporary "guitar" Roman Catholic mass as a means of validating Haydn's *Theresa Mass* is, in essence, no different from using Wagner and Nietzsche to validate Nazism—and vice versa in both cases.

The past illuminates the present. Although the present may bring into the light certain enshadowed aspects of the past, we must not select bits and pieces of the past solely to validate our contemporary prejudices, nor should we select bits and pieces of the past solely to be honored with our reflected glories. What the humanities, what the past, must do is shed a bright and steady illumination on the moment that we call Now. Spotlights and roman candles have their use—they select, they intensify, they color—but they do not illuminate.

The past, however, is only one prospect, only one view from the hill. Artists, poets, scholars (in the Emersonian sense) see more clearly than most people. They—or rather, their art—is more *grown-up* than most people are. And if, by now, you don't know what I mean by grown-up, I mean Shakespeare, most of all. I mean the artist who first sculptured Shiva Nataraja, I mean Jesus on the Mount, I mean Phidias. I mean not these people who are all now dead, but their art, which is alive. And new art has just as much permanence as art of the past, as well as much more built-in relevance for us. That is the reason for and the defense of the use of contemporary instances in humanities teaching. The modern arts provide an exciting, ready-to-wear lead-in to the universality of the human experience. Conversely, or maybe similarly, the classic arts provide an objective and dignified lead-in to the human experience. To exalt one or the other to preeminence is to miss the point of humanities, the universality of the human experience. Exaltation of the classic arts leads to making us into Miniver Cheevys, scornful of present-day man; but exaltation of the contemporary makes us mediocre journalists, scornful even of yesterday's man.

I fear I have gone far beyond brass tacks, and I am giving way to my instinctive style, of which I would say, with Christopher Morley:

> No bird has built an April nest
>
> More instinctive than my rhyme . . . .

Yet no writing is mere instinct, it is conscious art, too, and art is most successful when it communicates easily, is indiscernible from instinct. A ballet is most expressive when one is unconscious of physical effort and conscious art, for it is then that expression can be free, completely abstracted from the moment in time. That, by the way, is why humanist teachers must expose themselves and their students to the finest expressions in an art form. Rejection of all jazz, for example, can result from exposure to bad jazz, where people are conscious of the work involved, not their involvement in the work of art. That, though, is incidentally said; now to the matter at hand.

The matter at hand is methods of teaching the humanities. What may be hidden in my literary style is my art, for in this book I set out to make each chapter serve as an example of a different method of teaching. In every chapter, of course, I have tried directly to discuss an approach or method of teaching, as for example, American Studies, or popular culture, or literary criticism. In every chapter I also have deliberately used different techniques of teaching. Let me point to some of these.

In the first chapter, I made use of a current event (the moon landing) as a lead-in to discussion of humanities and values.

In the second chapter, I made use of "pure" history (the Renaissance) as a means of clarifying some essential definitions.

In the third chapter, I deliberately abused the interdisciplinary method by using a greater variety of sources than any teacher could bring comfortably into the classroom.

In the fourth chapter, I designed the essay to begin as a conversation (about my father-in-law), raised it to a discussion, and dissolved it at the end into conversation.

In the fifth chapter, I used commonplace art (the graffito) to arrive at the essentials of the creative impulse.

In the sixth chapter, I used extended definition (of metaphor, image, and symbol) as a means of developing tools for understanding literature.

In the seventh chapter, I provided specific professional and bibliographical references as a means of expanding a point (the importance and relevance of American Studies among the humanities).

In the eighth chapter, I provided a specific ready-made curriculum from my own experience in teaching, including a sample hand-out sheet.

In the ninth chapter, I related the humanities movement to analogous movements in other fields (medical general practice and ecology).

And in this chapter, I have frankly disclosed my hand to show my conscious artifice (above).

These are not the only methods that I have deliberately employed, but they should serve to show how a humanities teacher (and a humanist) must work: consciously making use of techniques ordinarily associated with other disciplines and with more disciplined others. Humanists—particularly those of the nine-months-to-immortality breed—do themselves ill-service if they disdain current events, pure history, conversation, commonplace art, careful definition, bibliography, hand-out sheets, analogy, and self-analysis.

Despite these varied methods, I am sure that my readers are aware of a notable sameness throughout the book. You cannot escape me, you cannot escape the personal anecdote, you cannot escape the follow-your-nose images, you cannot escape "these twigs and straws, / The casual shreds of every day" (Morley again). You cannot escape me because I, like the teacher in the classroom, hold the shreds together.

Teaching humanities is like wrestling an octopus: disunity and dissonance are inherent in the task. Whatever unity there can be to interdisciplinary studies ultimately must be individualistic. Egotistic. Humanistic. Man is our basic value; individual man who matters, every man who severally and eachly possesses self-respect; the ego, that is, who judges for himself, but judges from knowledge and experience, not from empty prejudice and turgid ignorance. The humanist, therefore, is in no position to deny his ego, or depreciate his own experience. What student can respect a teacher who wallows in humility and self-denial? What reader can follow a writer who says his opinion is valueless? The world grows better because of humanitarians, not humilitarians.

On the other hand (there always is another hand, as in a Hindu statue), ego-tinted as this book has been, and as a humanities classroom must be, its whole purpose has been an extended warning against narrow-minded purveying of ego-sanctioned truths. If humanities is to do any good in the world, it must dispel the infantile belief in the academic existence of the truth, the whole truth, and nothing but the truth. In short, my ego in this book does not establish a truth, nor does the teacher's ego in his classroom; but from my ego comes the art, not the mere craft of writing; and far more important, with the individual ego comes the true art of teaching, not mere methods.

In other words, what I am saying here is that the teacher must himself serve as a document in humanities. He must convey to his students that he is himself part and parcel of mankind, that he is involved in the whole human experience, not only as actor and creator, but as a knowledgeable audience, a culture consumer. This should not be conveyed overtly, by mouthy confessionals of name dropping or declarations of "philosophy of life," but by honest involvement in the content of the course. Content is important, because one of the humanities teacher's primary purposes is to broaden his students' cultural experience. Technique is important, too, because another of the teacher's primary purposes is to train students in techniques for understanding the world within which they live. Ego is important as well, because from the teacher's ego comes style, and it is style that raises teaching from craft to art. But if any of these three must go, let it be ego, because that is the only thing the student already has, unfinished though it may be. Moreover, he will meet egos aplenty, far more worthy than his teachers' and mine, as he encounters Socrates, Faulkner, Li Po, Franklin, Marx, Caravaggio, Dostoevsky, Voltaire, Caesar, and St. Francis.

These are strong personalities, and they represent some highly divergent viewpoints, not all of which are congenial to the teacher, his students, or their community. But the investigation of these personalities and their ideas does not require factional alliance with every point of view expressed. What is paramount is that the teacher be open-minded about every item he teaches, while he teaches it. This is actually a matter of "it's an interesting place to visit, but I wouldn't want to live there." The teacher and his students may visit Pericles' Athens, Murger's Paris, Savanarola's Florence, Haroun-al-Raschid's Baghdad, or Luther's Wittenberg, but they need not live there. Or try it this way: "It's interesting, but I wouldn't want it in my home." Hitler, after all, is fascinating, but we shouldn't like him as a guest in our homes. Or our world. This is true in the aesthetic realm, too; one may appreciate the Impressionists, and yet not wish to have them in his house.

The fact that one does have a choice of making various aesthetic and philosophical factions part of his own life points up the need for humanistic education. We have a bewildering variety of choices because we live in a world of mass production. Mass literacy began, in the Renaissance, with Gutenberg; mass art began at the same time with Schongauer and Dürer; music for mass audiences also began at roughly the same time, with the development of the pipe organ, though music was not really widely disseminated until the advent of Thomas Edison and the phonograph. A century ago, no one had the luxury of hearing a Brahms concert and having to deal with the problem of whether or not to have the First Symphony in his home. Humanities for every man are here, available right now; what humanities teachers must do is to make sure that humanities are not a shallow puddle of the present for the masses of men, with scattered clear deep pools reserved for the few.

Whether the clear deep pools are opened to every man all depends. It depends, first, on a broader interpretation than the elitist classics-Renaissance approach has allowed. It depends upon faith in the essential equality of man. It depends, too, upon hard-headed acceptance of the practical inequality of men. In our equality, all men share a common autobiography: We are born, alone; we live, no longer alone, with other men; and, we die, once more alone. But in details, we are different, for we are born in different places and times, we live by different means and for different goals, and we move toward our inevitable deaths by different roads. The equality of mankind, therefore, is real, but it is so sweeping and all-inclusive that only at certain rare moments of epiphany do we see the forest leaves part to afford us a crystal perspective in which at once infinity and variety are gathered together, like a view of our worlds in a convex mirror.

In my father's house there were many mansions, for I grew up among books, and pictures, and music, and dialogues, and love. Among these mansions was a window on the world just like this: a convex mirror in the Federal style, which, from little-boyhood—when I used to climb the chair to enter the mirror world in which all my father's mansions were reflected—on to the present time, has drawn me into the transcendent world of each-and-all. This mirror is surrounded by patriotic symbols and surmounted by an eagle. The gathering of infinity in the mirror's crystal perspective, is, as I said, but a parting of the leaves, a peep through the bewildering variety of our immediate worlds. But the mirror is encircled by equalitarian symbols, and more: it is a mass-produced reproduction. It is a humanistic, egocentric, sweeping prospect of every man's world—mine and yours—at popular prices. It is a distorted view of here-and-now, it is an altered image of I-here and out-there, and so it makes us see ourselves and our world with new, and heightened, and clarified sight. Although it is a mass-produced reproduction, although it is American, it is remote in time, and to many may seem as foreign and elite as Jan van Eyck's painting of a similar mirror in the *Arnolfini Wedding*. No matter, for everyone today can find the same world of each-and-all in a contemporary work of popular art, in Neil Armstrong's gleaming sun visor on the moon, in a chromium-plated automobile hubcap, or in a shiny doorknob. And when anyone sees himself mirrored in the larger perspective of other men's works, he has taken one step toward joining in the human race.

Appendix
Humanities Self-Taught:
A Selection of Readings

In preparing this list of books I have been governed by the needs of several kinds of readers, among them teachers in service who are now teaching humanities courses or are contemplating teaching humanities courses, but who have not had the benefit of an orderly course in the humanities; nonteachers of all ages who would like to build a basic library in the humanities; and professors and supervisors who are designing courses and workshops in humanities education. All the works listed are either anthologies or historical and critical works, and they should not be regarded as a substitute for complete primary sources. My purpose here is to provide the overview that can be gained from anthologies and histories, and the tools for understanding that develop from the use of critical works. I have generally avoided highly personal works, and wherever there has been a choice, I have selected standard works rather than unproven new works. I have also chosen inexpensive editions wherever these exist. Many of the books listed are commonly used as college texts, but I have not intended this to be a classroom list of teaching

147

materials. I have not listed any books mentioned in the body of my text.

One of the most complete collections of literature is *The World in Literature*, edited by George K. Anderson and Robert Warnock (Glenview, Ill., Scott, Foresman, 1967), which has been published in many formats since 1950. The introductory material is excellent, and the selections include oriental as well as Western works and philosophical and critical writings as well as *belles lettres*. This anthology, combined with *Art and Civilization* by Bernard S. Myers (New York, McGraw-Hill, 1967), provides a solid core of information and a rich body of resources in history, philosophy, literature, painting, and architecture. *Art and Civilization* includes oriental art and prehistoric and modern primitive arts and histories, and it is sumptuously illustrated. There are available many fine books similar to these, but most of them ignore the Orient or are thin on modern arts and literature.

A less expensive alternative is the three-volume paperback *Classics of Western Thought* (New York, Harcourt, Brace & World, 1964), compiled under the general editorship of Thomas H. Greer, who also wrote the complementary *Brief History of Western Man* (New York, Harcourt, Brace & World, 1968), which, in addition to well-chosen black and white illustrations, contains useful synoptic charts of achievements in religion, history, and the arts, and clear historic maps. The series title, "Classics of Western Thought," is accurate, for the selections are European and American, and emphasize standard works in political and social thought, although poetry, drama, and fiction are represented. The format of these books is not so overwhelming as that of those in the paragraph above.

Similar to Greer's *Brief History of Western Man* is *The Humanities Handbook*, by Joseph Satin (New York, Holt, Rinehart and Winston, 1969). Satin goes beyond a simple synopticon, and in his introductory chapter, "The Humanities Approach," he explains the comprehensive interdisciplinary thematic approach that runs throughout his chronology of Western civilization. This, unlike any of the foregoing books, includes discussions of musical history.

The most complete humanities approach in any textbook I have seen can be found in *The Search for Personal Freedom*, a two-volume collection written and edited by Neal M. Cross, Leslie Dae Lindou, and Robert C. Lamm (Dubuque, Iowa, William C. Brown Company, 1968). This contains not only major works of literature (for instance, *Oedipus the King*, Dante's *Inferno*, and *King Lear* complete) but also large color illustrations, musical scores, architectural diagrams, historical introductions, lessons in reading music from ancient Greek through modern jazz, indices of artistic symbols, glossaries, synopticons, bibliographies, and discographies—and a thematic organization!

The books listed above tend to be conservative and classical in approach, and they provide the traditional grounding in the humanities that is essential to understanding the humanities. In addition to this, they suggest patterns for integrating materials from different disciplines. For an example of how integration of traditional materials can be achieved through a single personality, there is Kenneth Clark's *Civilisation: A Personal View* (New York, Harper & Row, 1969) and, of course, Clark's television series with the same title. A broader approach than Kenneth Clark's is that of Jon D. Longaker, whose short textbook, *Art, Style, and History* (Glenview, Ill., Scott, Foresman, 1970) starts with a closely analyzed comparison of an African ancestral figure and a Greek statue of Zeus from the fifth century B.C., and proceeds chronologically and thematically throughout history with carefully selected individual examples that are analyzed in detail. It is well illustrated with diagrams and reproductions in color and in black and white, and it has rather scholarly project suggestions at the end of each chapter. A modern humanities anthology designed for use in high schools but useful to anyone interested in humanities is the "Voice of Man" series of paperbacks. One of the books in this series, subtitled *The Drinking Gourd*, edited by Vincent L. Medeiros, Jr., and Diana B. Boettcher (Menlo Park, Calif., Addison-Wesley Publishing Company, 1969), has included, along with modern poems and short stories, a television drama script, the music and lyrics of a Buffy St. Marie protest song, a Li'l Abner comic strip, and several color reproductions of contemporary paintings.

Keeping abreast of such current interests in the humanities and arts is difficult because authors and books come and go, but two particularly fine anthologies of first-rate theory and criticism that are likely to stay in print are *Modern Culture and the Arts*, edited by James B. Hall and Barry Ulanov (New York, McGraw-Hill, 1967), and *Aesthetics and the Arts*, edited by Lee A. Jacobus (New York, McGraw-Hill, 1968). Both include essays on film, dance, music, architecture, literature, and painting. Jacobus's book also has a good bibliography. There are today many anthologies that will introduce a reader to American black literature, but I think the best is one of the earliest, James A. Emanuel's and Theodore L. Gross's *Dark Symphony* (New York, The Free Press, 1968). It contains critical essays as well as poetry and fiction, and it has an exhaustive bibliography. As an introduction to the new American Indian as he relates to the humanities, *The American Indian Speaks*, edited by John R. Milton (Vermillion, S. Dak., University of South Dakota Press at Vermillion, 1969), manages in fewer than two hundred pages to give samples and statements from all of the arts. In history, the revolution that has been occurring in American historical studies since 1950 is summarized in a very readable one-volume history, *Out of Our Past*, by Carl N. Degler (New York, Harper & Row, 1959).

Extending our cultural and philosophical history into the present and the future is Theodore Roszak's *The Making of a Counter Culture* (New York, Doubleday, Anchor Books,

1969). This uneven but brilliant book may help adults to gain some understanding of current youth movements, including those that tie the humanities to oriental philosophies and ecological concerns. For a more detailed introduction to oriental philosophy, religion, and art, the best work is *Three Ways of Asian Wisdom* by Nancy Wilson Ross (New York, Simon and Schuster, 1966) and for science and the humanities, Rene Dubois's *So Human an Animal* (New York, Charles Scribner's Sons, 1968).

Two fields of humanistic study that have not yet produced satisfactory introductory works are popular culture and myth, although the books on popular culture mentioned in Chapter VIII are useful, and the *Journal of Popular Culture*, published at Bowling Green University in Ohio, will aid a reader in keeping up with the latest studies. Myth studies are going in all directions, but there is an attempt to draw all theories together in G. S. Kirk's rather esoteric *Myth: Its Meaning and Functions in Ancient and Other Cultures* (Berkeley, Calif., University of California Press, 1970). The best work for understanding classical myths and the literary works they have spawned over the past two millennia is Michael Grant's *Myths of the Greeks and Romans* (Cleveland, World Publishing Company, 1962).

Short pieces on creative self-expression are to be found in the anthologies mentioned above by Hall and Ulanov and by Jacobus; these could be supplemented in music with Virgil Thomson's *The State of Music*, which has been published in a revised edition (New York, Random House, Vintage Books, 1962). Contemporary creative art, particularly abstract painting and photography, is the subject of a long, expensive, and beautiful book written by Reid Hastie and Christian Schmidt. This is *Encounter with Art* (New York, McGraw-Hill, 1969). Of the many books on filmmaking, Kirk Smallman's *Creative Film-Making* (New York, Crowell-Collier and Macmillan, 1969) is, I think, the best, combining practical advice with clear-headed creative theory. The creative impulse in writing is the subject of much autobiographical literature and is to be found in nearly all of the anthologies I have mentioned, but I would add William M. Gibson's and George Arm's *Twelve American Writers*, (New York, Crowell-Collier and Macmillan, 1962), in which the editors have combined an extensive collection of creative selections with personal statements by the writers and critical commentaries by contemporaries and more recent writers.

Finally, for an authoritative study of the Italian Renaissance, the best books are Vincent Cronin's *The Florentine Renaissance* (New York, E. P. Dutton, 1967) and *The Flowering of the Renaissance* (New York, E. P. Dutton, 1969).

JOINING THE HUMAN RACE: How to Teach the Humanities is an attempt to unify the different directions and emphases of "the most dynamic force in American education today," the humanities movement - team teaching, modular scheduling, the inductive method, popular culture, the lively arts, minority studies, and nondirective teaching. If the two key words of the seventies are **relevance** and **inter-disciplinary,** all these new enthusiasms demand rigorous examination and exemplification in their light. This Professor Schroeder has done in these ten chapters.

◆ ◆ ◆

"The National Humanities Faculty can testify both to the excitement and the deep meaning which the humanities movement holds for the present and future of our society. We have for some time had in mind the potential to school and college people of just such a book as this, and we are pleased to have been able to lend it our support. For without being dogmatic in the least, Professor Schroeder sets forth a rationale for the humanities, points out a number of worthwhile directions which a program might take, and discusses honestly some of the traps laid for the unwary. It should be apparent that the author is a vibrant and devoted humanist who offers in this book the nourishing harvest of a unique set of experiences."